Corporate Financial Management

SUBSCRIPTION NOTICE

This Wiley product is updated on a periodic basis with supplements to reflect important changes in the subject matter. If you purchased this product directly from John Wiley & Sons, Inc., we have already recorded your subscription for this update service.

If, however, you purchased this product from a bookstore and wish to receive (1) the current update at no additional charge, and (2) future updates and revised or related volumes billed separately with a 30-day examination review, please send your name, company name (if applicable), address, and the title of the product to:

Supplement Department
John Wiley & Sons, Inc.
One Wiley Drive
Somerset, NJ 08875
1-800-225-5945

For customers outside the United States, please contact the Wiley office nearest you:

Professional & Reference Division
John Wiley & Sons Canada, Ltd.
22 Worcester Road
Rexdale, Ontario M9W 1L1
CANADA
(416) 675-3580
1-800-567-4797
FAX (416) 675-6599

John Wiley & Sons, Ltd.
Baffins Lane
Chichester
West Sussex, PO19 1UD
UNITED KINGDOM
(44) (243) 779777

Jacaranda Wiley Ltd.
PRT Division
P.O. Box 174
North Ryde, NSW 2113
AUSTRALIA
(02) 805-1100
FAX (02) 805-1597

John Wiley & Sons (SEA)
Pte. Ltd.
37 Jalan Pemimpin
Block B #05-04
Union Industrial Building
SINGAPORE 2057
(65) 258-1157

Corporate Financial Management

Strategies for Maximizing Shareholder Wealth

Earl S. Landesman

JOHN WILEY & SONS, INC.

New York • Chichester • Weinheim • Toronto • Singapore • Brisbane

This text is printed on acid-free paper.

Copyright © 1997 by Earl S. Landesman.
Published by John Wiley & Sons, Inc.

Library of Congress Cataloging-in-Publication Data:

Landesman, Earl S.
    Corporate financial management : strategies for maximizing
    shareholder wealth / Earl S. Landesman.
        p.   cm.
    Includes index.
    ISBN 0-471-12353-6 (cloth : alk. paper)
    1. Corporations—United States—Finance.   2. Strategic planning—
    United States.   I. Title.
    HG4061.L26   1996
    658.15—dc20   95-32070

Printed in the United States of America

10   9   8   7   6   5   4   3   2

Preface

During the past 20 years of working with the finance function, I have concluded that the success of a company is often contingent on the quality and leadership of finance.

As an auditor I observed that financial insolvency was closely tied to the neglect of financial management and its inability to confront business problems. While a member of a corporate finance staff, I was able to see the power that finance can wield over an organization. As a business consultant working with management to improve operations and business strategy, I saw the financial budgeting and forecasting processes getting in the way of efforts to improve business performance. Finally working with financial organizations and leading best practice studies for more than 10 years, I have come to appreciate that world-class financial leadership will drive world-class business performance.

Preface

While most companies recognize the importance of finance, efforts to improve finance's operating effectiveness and management leadership have been difficult and, at times, frustrating. Interest in implementing best practices has contributed to growing management expectations.

The application of best practices has highlighted the problem areas of finance. While the problem areas must be addressed, a case-by-case approach to improving financial functions and processes has resulted in suboptimal solutions and projects that are stymied by issues outside the limited scope of the financial reengineering project.

The tendency to emulate existing best practices often leads many companies to implement solutions for yesterday's competitive environment. Best practices should be seen as a springboard to improving the finance area. Financial reengineering must be driven by a financial leadership vision that begins with a bold mission: to maximize shareholder wealth.

Maximizing shareholder wealth requires a business orientation that is focused on growth and future success. Consequently, business initiatives must be developed and evaluated on their contribution to the long-term success of the business enterprise.

With a mission to maximize shareholder wealth, finance's fiduciary responsibility shifts from control to growth and innovation. Within this framework the continuous drum of corporate restructurings are challenged if their only objective is to reduce cost. Cost reduction alone is not enough. Short-term profit improvements cannot come at the expense of long-term business competitiveness.

The purpose of this book is to provide the CFO, financial leadership, and individual finance functions with the tools and framework to maximize shareholder wealth. It will provide you with direction and implementation strategies that will not only help your finance organization to become world-class but to define future world-class financial leadership.

I would like to thank a number of people who have contributed to the development of my thinking regarding financial and business

Preface

leadership: Richard Almeida, Robert Duffy, Bill McGrath, Robert Hoffman, Robert Frigo, George Hepburn, Mary Ann Doornbos, and Richard Flater. I would also like to thank a number of colleagues and clients who reviewed chapters and sections: Gary Williams, Julian M. Freedman, John F. Morrow, Alfred King, Fred Bleakley, and George Deputy.

I want to thank Sheck Cho from John Wiley & Sons. Sheck has worked with me through every step of the writing process. A special thanks to Erika Pendleton and Mary Daniello. Erika spent endless hours reviewing my manuscript, preparing it for production. Mary Daniello worked with me to keep the production of the book on schedule.

Finally, I would like to thank those who are committed to improving the effectiveness and leadership of finance. The desires and efforts of financial professionals to transform the finance function provide the motivation and energy of this book.

EARL S. LANDESMAN

Ann Arbor, Michigan
November 1996

Contents

Contents

Part Two   TRANSACTION PROCESSES

**Chapter 3   Supply Chain Model for Financial
                 Transaction Environment   47**

Contents

Contents

Contents

Contents

Contents

Contents

About the Author

Earl S. Landesman, CPA, is Chairman of Strategic Financial Partners, a financial and general management consulting firm committed to implementing leading-edge financial and business process solutions. Mr. Landesman has more than 20 years of industry and consulting experience. He has led financial benchmarking and best practices studies that involved the best financially managed corporations in America. He has worked with Fortune 500 corporations to implement financial best practices.

Mr. Landesman has published articles on financial and management topics and has been quoted in numerous publications including *Fortune*, *Business Week*, and *The Wall Street Journal*.

Prior to founding Strategic Financial Partners, Mr. Landesman was a Partner with Coopers & Lybrand L.L.P., Associate Partner with

About the Author

Andersen Consulting, and Principal at A.T. Kearney. In addition, he was on Chrysler Corporation's Corporate Finance staff during its 1980s turnaround.

Mr. Landesman has an MBA in Finance and Accounting from the University of Michigan and is a member of the AICPA.

Part One

CORPORATE FINANCIAL FRAMEWORK

CHAPTER 1

Defining the Twenty-First Century Finance Function

1.1 INTRODUCTION

The historical role of finance in companies has been the controllership function. This has traditionally included accounting, reporting, and transaction processing. Serving a controller, or "enforcer" function, finance has too often hindered operating performance by slowing the speed of business decisions and requiring multiple approvals and documentation that increase the cost of financial transactions.

Traditionally, the finance manager has not worked closely with operating management to improve business performance. This enabled the creation of a bureaucratic culture and contributed to a management information environment that provided little business information or insight. In the future, finance's value will be measured based on its contribution to business performance and shareholder wealth.

If this viewpoint is applied, the role of the finance function shifts from controlling to supporting management's efforts to improve business results. In other words, the primary role of the finance function will be to service the business. Proactive financial leadership must view service as a core value of the finance organization. Accordingly, finance must be managed as a supplier of financial services. Service-provider perspective requires that finance treat itself as a business—pricing services for a competitive market environment.

If the finance function is able to fill the need for better and more sophisticated analysis, financial management will play an increasingly important role in operating and strategic decisions. This role will allow the financial manager to build a close business partnership with key leaders of the business. Finance organizations that are not able to make this transition will become a serious drag on companies' ability to compete in the twenty-first century. Exhibit 1-1 highlights the core elements of the twenty-first century organization.

1.2 BUSINESS PROCESS INTEGRATION

Many leading companies are now moving to integrate their business processes through reengineering. Driven by the need to reduce costs, decrease time to market, and improve quality, business process reengineering integration is challenging the basic logic and rationale of the finance function. Business process reengineering integration focuses on how to manage getting a job done. Companies are integrating functional activities into a business process structure. This leads to the sharing or migration of financial activities. Integration shifts a manager's focus from functional to process management, and, as a result, discrete financial functions, such as accounts payable or collections, may be transferred to a business process manager, diminishing the financial manager's role in these functions and the size of the finance function itself. If outsourcing is combined with business

Exhibit 1-1   The Core Elements of the Twenty-First Century Finance Organization

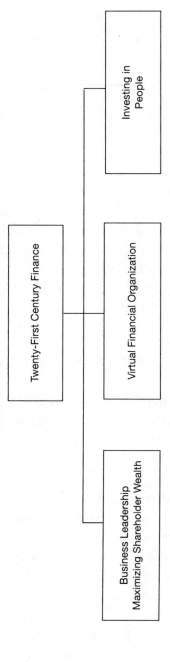

process management, the majority of current financial activities may be transferred out of finance for companies that use these techniques aggressively.

1.3 INTERNAL CONTROL ENVIRONMENT

As financial activities are pushed out to process managers, the finance manager's responsibilities will be tested. The strength of the internal control environment will play a critical role in management's ability to meet its fiduciary duty. The chief financial officer will continue to be ultimately accountable for the integrity of financial results, but this individual will have less control over the operational areas of finance. In this environment, fiduciary responsibilities and a commitment to protect and enhance shareholder value will increase substantially vis-à-vis the remaining responsibilities of finance.

1.4 OPERATING STRUCTURE

Proactive financial managers are responding to the challenge. They are radically rethinking the role and operating structure of the finance function. The restructuring of the finance function is being driven by a number of factors, including:

- Pressures to downsize
- The desire to reengineer the finance function from a clean-sheet perspective
- More outsourcing
- New information systems technology
- Business process integration

Business partnership and operation-driven management approach to financial transactions will be critical to successfully creating this new environment. This dual approach is transforming the role and perception of finance. It is evolving from a staff-oriented support function to a line and general management organization. However, the transformation of finance depends on its ability to serve as a business partner. Business partnership cannot be fully achieved without access to timely and quality information.

(a) DOWNSIZING

Beginning in the 1960s, companies began to fight the growth of bloated, centralized staffs. Decentralization was used to break up the monolithic financial accounting and transaction processing organizations. However, decentralization did not solve the problem of bloated centralized finance staffs; instead, it led to the proliferation of financial organizations, tripling and quadrupling the cost of finance. The recent trend toward downsizing has forced companies to reconsider the benefits of centralizing the finance function.

To benefit from decentralization and, at the same time, cut costs, companies are beginning to centralize accounting and transactional operations (e.g., accounts payable, billing, and payroll) and manage them as a shared service. Under a shared-service concept, the central operation is structured and managed to service the needs of the users. Success of shared-service management is measured on both customer satisfaction and cost. These organizations are essentially managed from a supplier-customer relationship. Many of the companies that have implemented shared services have realized cost savings ranging between 25 percent and 50 percent, with improved customer satisfaction. The cost savings are being realized as a result of consolidation, scale economies, and standardization of practices and systems.

A unique aspect of these operations is that world-class manufacturing practices are applied. Management is focused on productivity and quality. Self-directed work teams, quality circles, flexible work hours, and low-cost locations are just a few of the tools used to manage these low-cost operations.

(b) CLEAN-SHEET REENGINEERING

Clean-sheet reengineering is a process that obliterates many of the traditional activities of finance. For example, through clean-sheet reengineering, management might remove the following:

- Excessive approval levels and procedures
- Customer billing
- Vendor invoices
- Checks for payments
- Monthly closings
- Monthly forecasts
- Cost accounting

The cost savings range from 25 percent to 75 percent, and some companies have realized continuous productivity improvements exceeding 8 percent year after year. These ongoing savings are being driven by a commitment to quality and a management focus on the value of financial services.

(c) OUTSOURCING

Those companies that are unable to dramatically reduce financial operating cost can find others who will be happy to do it for them. If low cost is not feasible in-house, management can achieve significant savings by outsourcing the high-cost accounting and transaction processing operations, typically representing more than 60 percent of total financial operating cost, to an outside supplier.

With the growing use of credit cards for business purchasing, out-sourcing has taken on a new face. Using credit cards, referred to as purchasing cards, companies can achieve savings that exceed the total cost of their financial operations. In addition to the savings, access to real-time transaction information is now a reality.

(d) INFORMATION SYSTEMS TECHNOLOGY

Information systems technology and data architecture concepts are now coming of age with the ability to integrate information across the business world. With technology now able to integrate and provide real-time access to information, the infrastructure is in place to support the virtual corporation. Every time the Internet is referenced regarding a business service or product, one is witnessing "real time"—the building of the virtual corporation and virtual marketplace.

The leading financial organizations in the United States view information management as one of the top three priorities of their organizations. These companies realize that finance's value is limited to the timeliness and quality of analysis and business insight. Without an integrated management information architecture, finance will find that its leadership role is severely undermined.

As we move into the twenty-first century, with dramatic reduction in the large-cost centers of finance, attention will be shifted to the value-adding activities of finance. These costs will become higher as the overall cost of finance declines.

Senior financial executives will be under increasing pressure to deliver visible results or be challenged to reduce traditional financial-planning activities by similar levels as above.

While the need for finance to support management is more important than ever in today's cost-competitive environment, financial planning and decision support will be under pressure to improve productivity and reduce cycle times.

If finance is able to fill the need for better and more sophisticated analysis, financial management will play an increasingly important role in operating and strategic decisions. This role will allow finance to build a close business partnership with the key leaders of the business.

Information technology and data architecture concepts are now coming of age to provide finance with the information and decision support tools to meet the above requirements. Information technology can integrate information globally, across business units and functions, and between companies.

Combining business process management with state-of-the-art technology, we now have the business framework for the twenty-first century virtual corporation (see exhibit 1-2).

The emergence of the twenty-first century virtual finance organization must ultimately be linked to shareholder wealth. While this might be an odd concept, there are hard business reasons for it: (1) to prevent unbridled investment in state-of-the-art technology, (2) to provide a sound business basis to prioritizing investments and rationalizing resources, and (3) to assure that when all is said and done corporate efforts result in building the foundation for sustainable competitive advantage and for maximizing shareholders' return on their invested capital.

1.5   SHAREHOLDER WEALTH

The major difference between the financial markets and finance's benchmark of business and financial performance is shareholder value versus shareholder wealth. The financial markets are making evaluations of a company's future based on current knowledge and perceptions of the company and trends, including economics, technology, industry, and competition. In the case of shareholder wealth, fi-

Exhibit 1-2 Defining the Operating Environment for the Twenty-First Century Finance Organization

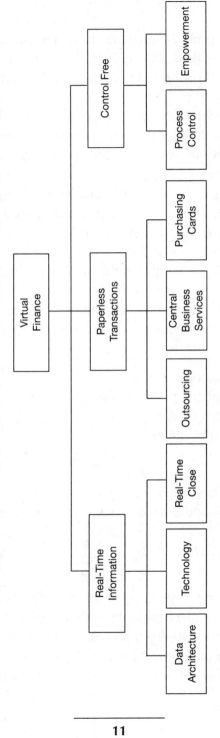

. . . Technology, benchmarking, and innovative best practices are leading us to conclude that the brave new world of the Virtual Corporation is inevitable.

11

nance is looking beyond the financial market's time horizon to consider long-term viability and growth. Theoretically, shareholder wealth should be fully reflected in today's market valuation—shareholder value.

From a pure discounted cash-flow perspective, a strategic investment might be considered a poor investment. However, if the company is successful twenty years from the date of the investment due to that strategic decision, it is the right decision. Only a generational or long-term view of creating future wealth would permit such an investment. This, however, should not be so surprising, since many privately held companies are willing to make such investments. These owners are concerned not only about their current dividends, but equally if not more with the financial future of their children and grandchildren to be.

With this strategic, long-term perspective in place, the major drivers of shareholder wealth, modeled in exhibit 1-3, include:

1. Market valuation
   - Current period performance
   - Confidence in management
   - Future expectations
2. Dividends
3. Financing and capital structure
4. Tomorrow's shareholder requirements
   - Financial and business risk impact on shareholder capital
   - Strategic investments

This is the highest-level view of shareholder wealth. The challenge for finance is to manage the levers that influence these drivers. Exhibit 1-4 begins the drill-down process for market valuation to emphasize that the major drivers of shareholder wealth will ultimately link to levers that can be controlled, planned, and managed. Share-

Exhibit 1-3 Shareholder Wealth Model

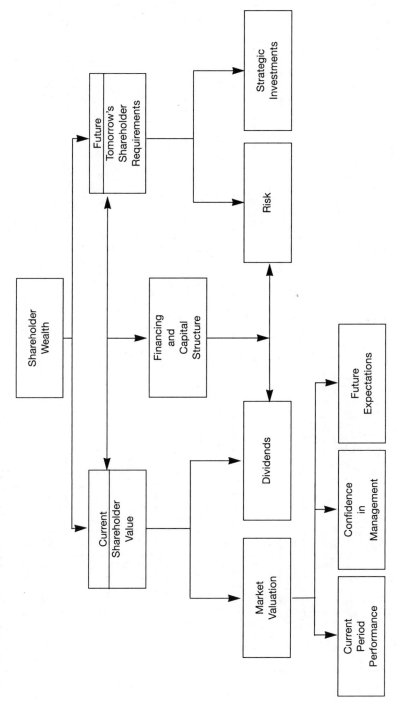

Exhibit 1-4 Shareholder Value Model

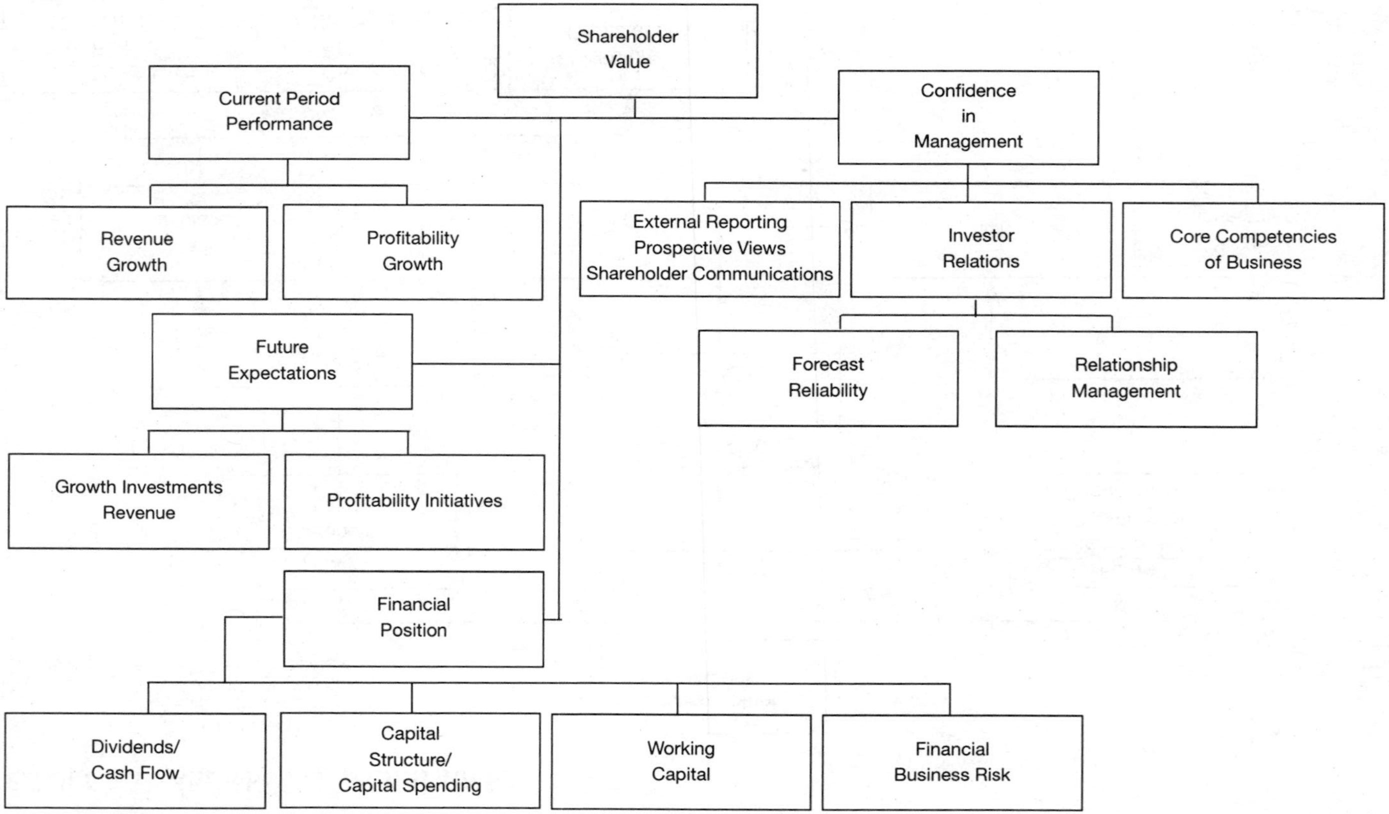

14

holder wealth has a much broader context for finance. Shareholder wealth begins with a view of time that bridges generations of shareholders and employees.

The view that management must take into consideration how today's decisions will strategically influence future wealth requires that managers balance their careers—dividing today's pressures on maximizing shareholder value against the best interests of the shareholders' future requirements, which the market will not normally factor into today's market value.

Shareholder wealth must become a guiding principle for finance. Maximizing shareholder wealth, which influences management and reengineering of finance, is an underlying premise throughout this book.

The twenty-first century finance organization will evolve into the general management structure of the business enterprise. This operating model for finance emphasizes shareholder wealth as a primary objective of financial reengineering, fusing all of finance's activities to managing business performance.

When combined with finance's view of the business that spans across all the activities of the enterprise, this move to a general management orientation will be a natural evolution, resulting in a fundamental transformation of the finance organization in the twenty-first century.

1.6   CONFIDENCE TO MEET THE FUTURE

A world-class finance organization is critical to the long-term sustainability of a world-class business enterprise. Further, financial managers who are committed to maximizing shareholder wealth and to delivering world-class financial and operating performance will have a clear sense that their role and mission is the business of working more effectively with operating management to create competitive ad-

Exhibit 1-5   Finance Plan 2000

	Major Initiatives	Results
Phase I—Eliminating Transaction Processing		
• Outsourcing transactions and systems	Purchasing cards	• Reduce overhead cost by 3% of purchases.
• Employee empowerment		
Phase II—Establishing Common Systems and Data Architecture		
• Globalization	Global shared services	• Reduce financial systems and operating cost by 25%.
		• Improve quality and access to information.
• Integrating supply chain	Process-oriented software	• Allow activity analysis and supported supply chain initiatives.
		• Improve competitiveness and increase sales.
Phase III—Business Leadership		
• Action-based budgeting	Budget tied to shareholder wealth	• Increase reliability of forecast and commitments to shareholders, resulting in increase in price/earnings ratio.
• Process management and core competencies	Restructured around process and core competency	• Improve profitability and increase revenues dramatically.

Year 2001—The Virtual Corporation

vantage and help position the future direction of the company to maximize shareholder wealth.

Exhibit 1-5 highlights the major initiatives that will create the twenty-first century finance organization. The path can take one to three years, but the benefits and the rewards will make the journey exciting and gratifying.

CHAPTER 2

Implementation Strategy and Methodology

2.1 ESTABLISHING A LEADERSHIP AGENDA

Downsizing, outsourcing, and the blurring of traditional roles and responsibilities of finance demand that the chief financial officer take a leadership role in setting the agenda for the finance function. Given the rapid changes taking place, the chief financial officer must reshape finance to be a cost-competitive supplier of financial services.

The chief financial officer must develop an operating strategy and organization that is customer-driven. The process to develop a leadership strategy will require (1) creating an environment to assure success (see exhibit 2-1) and (2) managing the process as a development of marketing strategy focused on delivering tangible results (see exhibit 2-2). The following are the key steps in establishing a market strategy for finance.

Exhibit 2-1 Creating an Environment for Success

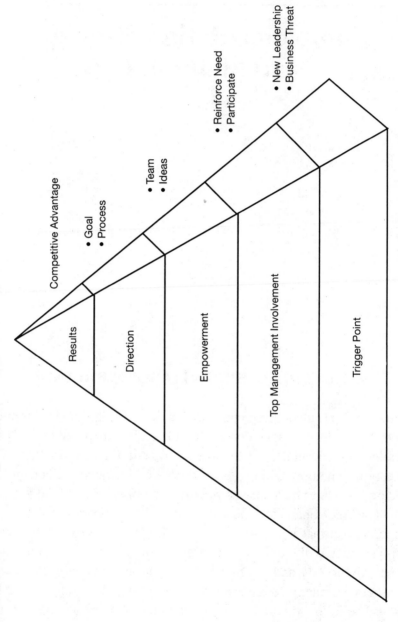

Exhibit 2-2 Developing a Financial Leadership Agenda

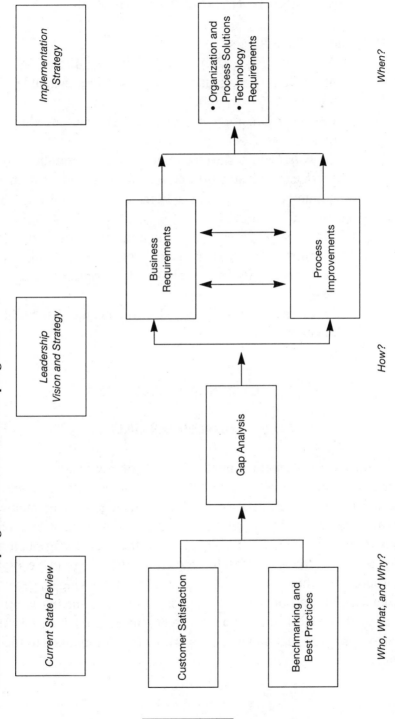

21

1. Current State Review
   - *Benchmarking.* Compare the services offered by the finance function against the best services available in the market.
   - *Customer satisfaction.* Define customers' needs and requirements.
   - *Gap analysis.* Develop an unbiased calibration of today's services against world-class practices and customer requirements and identify actions required to meet goals.
2. Vision and Strategy
   - *Leadership vision.* Develop a vision that is grounded in a commitment that financial reengineering will improve business results and emphasize the priorities of the business.
   - *Implementation strategy.* Deliver results that build momentum.

2.2 CURRENT STATE REVIEW

(a) BENCHMARKING

A financial management framework based on my Stages of Business Transformation can be used to define world-class attributes and create a basis for establishing an effective change management program. A company can be identified as functioning primarily at one of four levels, or stages of excellence, with the fourth stage being the highest standard. A successful reengineering program recognizes that individual functions and leaders will be at varying stages of excellence. This can be used to emphasize that a company is only as good as its weakest link. Therefore, reengineering must be a comprehensive program that moves all departments and functions to the next stage.

2.2 Current State Review

An overview of these Stages of Business Transformation is presented in exhibit 2-3. This organizational framework shows that businesses and their organizations move through stages of development. These stages are characterized by unique attributes that people can easily identify:

- Stage 1 focuses on transaction processing and meeting today's requirements. This stage lacks control capabilities, and as control improves, the organization moves into Stage 2.
- Stage 2 has tight financial controls, with a focus on meeting budgets and adhering to policies and procedures. The bureaucratic mentality that sometimes results from such a focus can lead to less than optimal performance. Therefore, breakthrough in performance is the key to reaching Stage 3.
- Stage 3 is characterized by functional excellence, with the focus on business decisionmaking. Although finance operates as a business partner with other functions, parochialism can stem from "functional silos" and constrain overall company performance.
- Stage 4 requires a business process focus, resulting in finance becoming a fully integrated team member working on common objectives and focusing on value-added initiatives.
- Stage 5 creates a financial control and transaction environment, leveraging technology to create the virtual corporation.

An organization moves from stage to stage as a result of internal or external pressures to change—trigger points. The trigger can consist of new leadership or dramatic changes in the business environment. Benchmarking itself often serves as a trigger point because it identifies practices that have been demonstrated as the most beneficial. A successful transition results in dramatic changes in business practices and policies.

Exhibit 2-3 Stages of Business Transformation/Financial Leadership—An Organizational Revolution

Major Attributes	Entrepreneur	Command and Control	Quality	Business Integration	Twenty-First Century
Business character	• Day to day	• Small leadership group • Top down	• Functional/technical excellence	• Process management	• Virtual
Finance role	• Transaction processor/"bean counter"	• Controller/bureaucrat	• Business partner	• Change agent	• Shareholder advocate
Business challenge	• Chaos	• Inflexibility	• Uneven improvement	• Multiple roles and responsibilities	• Empowerment and accountability

Finance challenges	• Establishing controls
	• Developing tactical plans
	• Identifying/managing resource requirements
	  • budgets
	  • costing
		• Understanding customer requirements
		• Comparing to world class
			• Understanding business requirement
			• Providing timely and relevant business information
				• Building core competencies
				• Serving business based on value: cost and service
					• Creating a control-free environment
					• Designing an intervention-free virtual information environment

Identification of a company's stage offers management an opportunity to discuss the strengths and weaknesses of the finance function and to understand the critical attributes of the next stage. People easily relate to the terms and quickly identify issues and business processes that correlate with their stage of organizational development. The concept provides a path forward—a path that recognizes both the organization's current capabilities and the attributes of a world-class organization.

(i)   Benchmarking Framework

Each function of finance can be analyzed in a framework that allows comparison of a finance organization against the world-class costs and practices of the best finance organizations. Benchmarking and best practices are integral to every step of the financial transformation process.

Best practices are characteristics or attributes that contribute to world-class performance, such as:

- Lowering cost
- Improving productivity
- Reducing cycle time
- Improving quality
- Enhancing value

All aspects of the process, function, product, or business area under review that contribute to substantial improvements in performance are within the realm of best practices. The challenge is measuring net contribution. For instance, too often technology is viewed as a best practice productivity solution, which in fact may turn out to be a detriment.

A case in point is the use of optical scanning to process payments. At first glance it looks like a great solution to lower the labor cost associated with handling transactions, but the technology also serves as an enabler for the continuation of a process that should be eliminated. Best practices must be assessed against achieving the ideal future state. Anything short of this could become an enabler for the "old ways of doing business" and cement poor business practices into a company's infrastructure permanently.

Exhibit 2-4 provides an example of how benchmarking and best practices support each step of the reengineering process.

Exhibit 2-5 provides an analytical framework for conducting a benchmarking and best practices evaluation. This framework links the evaluation to contribution to business and financial performance. Throughout this book, financial reengineering will focus on improving business and financial performance. This forces the intellectual discipline to present a coherent plan that demonstrates how improvements in finance will result in improvements to the business. Benchmarking and best practices will provide us with the trigger point to successfully challenge current paradigms and the "old ways of doing business," and the metrics to calibrate today's performance and legitimately identify the potential for improvement (see exhibit 2-6).

(ii) Benchmarking Cost

The first step in the benchmarking process is to analyze cost. The cost of corporate and operating unit finance is evaluated in total and by function. Cost is an indicator of both efficiency and effectiveness. High cost typically is an indicator of excessive approval requirements and bureaucratic procedures. High cost serves as a red flag during an assessment of a finance organization. A key driver of finance cost is operating structure. For example, decentralization can increase finance costs by 300 percent to 400 percent. This is a major factor that has led companies to reduce these costs by establishing centralized shared services.

An overview of the cost mix of finance and the key cost drivers is

Exhibit 2-4   Creating a World-Class Finance Function

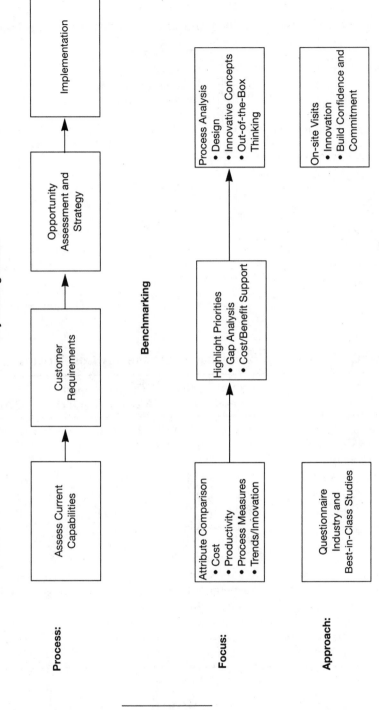

Key Building Blocks

Process:

| Assess Current Capabilities | → | Customer Requirements | → | Opportunity Assessment and Strategy | → | Implementation |

Benchmarking

Focus:

Attribute Comparison
• Cost
• Productivity
• Process Measures
• Trends/Innovation

→

Highlight Priorities
• Gap Analysis
• Cost/Benefit Support

→

Process Analysis
• Design
• Innovative Concepts
• Out-of-the-Box Thinking

On-site Visits
• Innovation
• Build Confidence and Commitment

Approach:

Questionnaire Industry and Best-in-Class Studies

Exhibit 2-5 Benchmarking and Best Practices Evaluation Framework

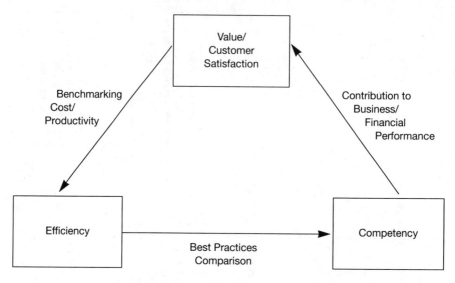

Exhibit 2-6 Cost Mix of Finance and the Key Cost Drivers

	Accounting and Transactions	Corporate and Business Support	Corporate
Average % Mix of Financial Operating Cost:	55–60%	30–40%	4–8%
Primary Activities:	Accounts payable Accounts receivable Billing Credit and collection General accounting Payroll	Cost accounting Financial planning and analysis	Audit Tax Treasury External reporting
Key Drivers:	Processing volume	Business structure	Management style

provided in exhibit 2-6. The first step in maximizing the effectiveness of a company's resources and investment is to evaluate the financial operating cost mix against processing productivity (e.g., transactions per employee) and cost per transaction. This is based on an evaluation of each function against a variety of costs, including:

- Employment
- Systems
- Overhead
- Contract services

(iii)   Financial Practices

Management's requirements of finance go beyond the need for a low-cost supplier. Management needs a finance organization that contributes to business performance through:

- Business partnership
- Financial talent with world-class analytical capabilities
- Strong financial leadership able to challenge and lead
- Technical excellence
- Timely and reliable information

The ability to deliver these capabilities can be benchmarked against the practices of the best financial organizations. The key areas to be evaluated in measuring performance and leadership for functional excellence are:

- Day-to-day management
- Career and professional development
- Continuous improvement/quality program
- Leveraging/sharing of services
- Centers of excellence

The key areas to be evaluated in measuring performance and leadership for business partnership are:

- Information management
- Decision support
- Contribution to business results

Each functional category can be examined to assess a finance organization against the Stages of Business Transformation. For example, to move from a Stage 2 bureaucratic, control-oriented environment to Stage 3, finance should focus its efforts on functional excellence, probably by developing strong leaders through active career management and investment in training and development. These leaders will have broad financial and operating experience and will have moved through divisions and the corporation with international experience. They should be individuals who are willing to stand up and challenge current thinking in order to improve business performance and shareholder value.

(iv) Financial Information Environment

A critical infrastructure requirement to reaching Stage 3 or Stage 4 is financial information. The majority of financial systems are unable to provide decision support capabilities. The goal is to develop a management information environment that:

- Integrates financial and operating data, providing finance with the tools to provide analysis and decision support for a company's value-added chain. Exhibit 2-7 highlights how the major financial activities support the core business processes.
- Provides for profit-and-loss and balance-sheet analysis by any view management wishes. Exhibit 2-8 illustrates a world-class information-rich financial information environment.

Exhibit 2-7 Financial Integration of the Value Chain

Column phases: Demand Generation | Procure | Create | Deliver | Service

Disbursements
- Accounts Payable — Cost of Purchased Products & Services
- Payroll — Employment Cost
- Travel & Expenses — Employee Expenses

Revenue
- Credit — Credit Authorization & Sale Value
- Billing — Price of Product & Service
- Collections — Balance Due
- Cash Application — Cash Received

Financial & Management Information
- Financial Accounting — Reporting of Financial Results
- Capital/Fixed Assets — Depreciation, Amortization, Asset Cost
- Tax Planning & Compliance — Tax Expense & Liability
- Internal Audit/ Business Controls — Integrity of Business Processes and Reliability of Financial Information

Strategic Financial Management
- Cost & Profitability Management — Costing of Products, Services & Business Processes
- Performance Management — Operating & Financial Metrics—Leading Indicators & Drivers of Financial & Operating Performance
- Cash & Working Capital Management — Optimizing Cash Flow & Short-Term Financing Requirements
- Budgeting & Forecasting — Action Plans to Improve Financial & Business Performance
- Corporate Finance — Financing of Capital Expenditures to Support Operations

Exhibit 2-8 Foundation for World-Class Financial Information Environment

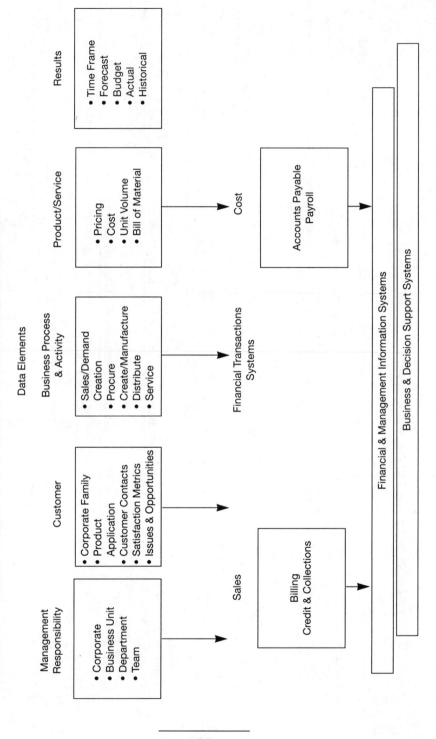

(b) CUSTOMER SATISFACTION

Comparing a finance function against the best finance organizations is only the beginning of developing a world-class finance function. No matter what the inherent capabilities of the organization, the finance function ultimately must be measured by its ability to satisfy the customer. The customer consists of both internal users of services (e.g., managers who need financial information to support decision making or departments that need timely and low-cost processing of transactions) and purchasers of the company's products or services. Customers are looking for value—the lowest cost for the desired products and service levels. Understanding customer requirements is essential for maximizing the value of finance's contribution to the business.

Transition to a new stage requires rethinking practices from both clean-sheet and external viewpoints. Process reengineering provides the clean-sheet methodology; customer satisfaction provides the external viewpoint.

You will never know what management or business customers want until you ask them. In fact, that is exactly what leading financial organizations are doing. Finance is now asking what their customers want and measuring operating performance against the responses. Many companies survey their customers annually, and they have developed quality measures and cost targets that are measured monthly.

(c) GAP ANALYSIS

The gap analysis will be a challenge. Clear documentation and benchmarking of cost, practices, and customer requirements can easily be developed. The challenge for financial management is to see itself objectively and develop an unbiased calibration of today's services and practices against world-class practices and customer requirements.

This analysis must be done with broad financial and operating management collaboration.

Operating management must be involved in this assessment to assure that finance stays focused on developing recommendations that will help management improve business and financial performance.

2.3   VISION AND STRATEGY

(a)   LEADERSHIP VISION

In response to the gap analysis, a leadership vision must be established to address:

- Roles and responsibilities of financial management
- Cost and customer performance targets
- Organizational and systems requirements
- Professional and career development
- Prioritization of business process improvements

Actions must be driven by top management commitment to a leadership vision. This vision must address the needs of all the constituencies of finance:

- Business management
- Finance employees
- Shareholders

A vision must be grounded in a commitment to improving business results and must be integrated into the priorities of the business. A logical area for integration of a finance improvement program is a company's quality management program. A world-class organization and a quality-driven organization are synonymous. A finance program linked to quality will receive the support of the organization. Most important, a quality linkage recognizes a long-term commitment to the following goals:

- Continuous improvement
- Customer satisfaction

(b)   IMPLEMENTATION STRATEGY

Establishing a vision is only the beginning. Implementation must be led by a management team committed to change and willing to be measured and held accountable for results. This management team must have a personal character reflected by the stage of transformation that is to be achieved. Exhibit 2-9 emphasizes that the project team must have strong leadership, a tool kit, and a communications strategy.

Once a management team is in place, the focus must shift to ac-

Exhibit 2-9   Project Team Requirements

Leadership	• Focus on business requirements • Establish team ownership for project recommendations and success • Challenge outdated paradigm • Involve and reinforce top management's support • Active and open communications
Tool Kit	• Definition of "Best in Class" • Best practices • Cost/performance metrics
Communication	• Ongoing and open communications • Clear understanding of objectives and expectations

tion. Exhibit 2-10 emphasizes that a comprehensive action plan must be developed to prioritize opportunities and address:

- Action required
- Timing
- Investment
- Expected results and benefits

It is important to focus resources on opportunities that will provide the greatest cost/benefit relationship and early successes to build momentum. The following are examples of how to identify and prioritize opportunities for improvement:

- Changes that are critical to support strategic initiatives and increase customer satisfaction
- Quick fixes that are independent of organizational and systems changes and are easy to implement
- Highly visible changes that send a clear message to the organization and demonstrate management's commitment to improvement
- Redundant or non-value-added activities that can be quickly eliminated
- Cost-saving opportunities that can "fund" further investment

Change is never ending and must be managed. But the early stages of an improvement program can be chaotic and must be managed with clear direction and focus. The following are critical for success:

- Manage change with the same intensity as you use to manage day-to-day operations.
- Achieve early, visible successes, communicate them, and share credit across the organization.

Exhibit 2-10 Implementation Strategy—Comprehensive Plan

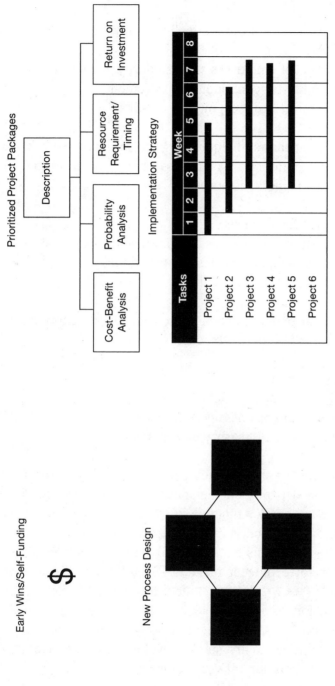

Early Wins/Self-Funding

Prioritized Project Packages

Description

Cost-Benefit Analysis

Probability Analysis

Resource Requirement/ Timing

Return on Investment

Implementation Strategy

Tasks	Week							
	1	2	3	4	5	6	7	8
Project 1								
Project 2								
Project 3								
Project 4								
Project 5								
Project 6								

New Process Design

Project Management
- Decision-Making Protocol
- Setting Expectation
- Reward System for Team

- Promote teamwork and a feeling of ownership throughout the process.
- Empower all employees with authority, responsibility, and accountability for continuous improvement.
- Tie appraisal and recognition to results.

Change is not easy and requires significant investment of management time, but building a world-class finance organization will deliver improved business results by providing:

- Low-cost financial services
- Information and analysis that improve decision making
- Technical support and insight that directly improve the financial results of the business

Taking a similar path, this book approaches the transformation of finance as a series of building blocks.

- Transaction processing
- Information management
- Financial and business performance
- Shareholder and treasury management

Exhibit 2-11 illustrates that each phase of building a world-class finance function depends on the foundation. Accordingly, this book will examine the finance function in the same sequence that must be taken to build a world-class finance organization.

A major goal of this book is to provide the confidence, process, and direction to reengineer finance. The following financial reengineering guide (see exhibit 2-12) identifies the major items that must be addressed for each major element of the financial reengineering process. As you evaluate the reengineering implications of a chapter, refer to this guide as the first step in developing a reengineering initiative and process solution for your company.

Exhibit 2-11 Building a Strong Foundation

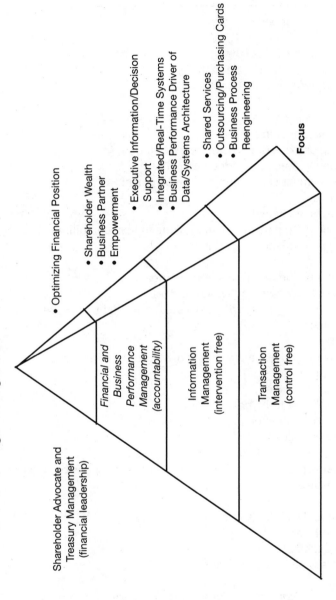

- Optimizing Financial Position

- Shareholder Wealth
- Business Partner
- Empowerment

- Executive Information/Decision Support
- Integrated/Real-Time Systems
- Business Performance Driver of Data/Systems Architecture

- Shared Services
- Outsourcing/Purchasing Cards
- Business Process Reengineering

Focus

Shareholder Advocate and Treasury Management (financial leadership)

Financial and Business Performance Management (accountability)

Information Management (intervention free)

Transaction Management (control free)

Core Processes (objective)

Exhibit 2-12   Reengineering Project Guide

Reengineering is not new.
What's new:
- Business Success Paradigm
  - empowerment and accountability
  - total customer satisfaction
  - speed
- Design Objectives
  - cross-functional integration
  - meeting or exceeding customer expectations
  - eliminating non-value-added activities
- Top Management Leadership and Involvement
  - proactive
  - encouraging change
  - empowering organization and linking to accountability
  - setting performance expectations

Define the intent and objectives of reengineering.
- Redesigning processes, activities, and jobs
- Aligning responsibilities with process and highlighting process core competencies
  - alignment
    - business process team or organization
    - restructuring
  - core competencies
    - yes: invest to be best in class
    - no: outsource or shared services
- Changing the rules
  - reducing traditional controls and bureaucracy
  - increasing process team's accountability and responsibility for results
- Changing corporate culture

Before starting, develop a game plan.
Strategy for success
Project management
Process focused on tangible results

. . . Consensus, Consensus, Consensus, Consensus
Organizational Buy-In Is Essential

Exhibit 2-12   *(Continued)*

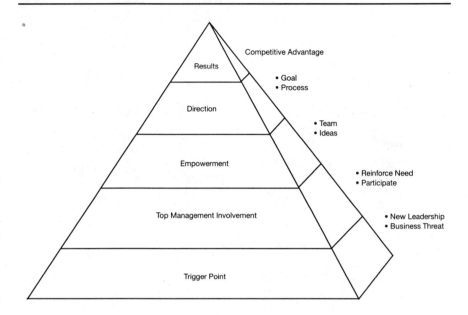

Leadership	• Focus on business requirements
	• Establish team ownership for project recommendations and success
	• Challenge outdated paradigm
	• Involve and reinforce top management's support
	• Active and open communications
Tool Kit	• Definition of "Best in Class"
	• Best practices
	• Cost/performance metrics
Communication	• Ongoing and open communications
	• Clear understanding of objectives and expectations

Exhibit 2-12   *(Continued)*

Getting Started—Establishing a Leadership Team
Steering Committee
- Define the purpose of the project
- State reason for action
- Set expectations
  - benefits
  - breakthrough thinking
  - project team responsibilities

Project Team
- Empowerment to break paradigms
- Members respected throughout the organization
- Cross-functional representation

Current State Review of Finance
Financial Functions/Processes Assessment
- Mission and goals
- Activities and primary products and services
  - How many people and resources are devoted to each activity?
  - How often do you do them?
- What is the trigger or cause of the activities?
  - What are the key business processes that these activities support?
- Major customers and what they need
  - What are the products or services provided to each major customer?
- Drivers of excessive work or non-value-added work
- What would they do to improve your effectiveness of your function and to meet or exceed your customers' expectations?

Current State Review—Business Requirements
Customer Interview
- What are the mission and goals of the process or department you manage?
- What are the biggest challenges facing the company and your responsibility area today and 3–5 years from now?
- How is finance helping your organization/process and the company to address these challenges?

Exhibit 2-12   *(Continued)*

- What products and services do you receive from finance?
- Why do you receive these products and services?
- How do you use these products and services?
- Are you satisfied with quality and timeliness?
- What changes would you recommend to improve finance ability to you and the company?

Gap Analysis
What are the major gaps?
- Process—cost, timing, core competencies
  - What are the non-value-added activities?
  - What are the major drivers of cost and noncompliance?
  - Who are the customers (departments and processes)?
  - What are the major customer service measures and how well do existing products and services meet the customer needs?
  - How do the process and activities compare with benchmarks and best practices?
- Customer satisfaction—describe
  - What do our customers need?
  - How and when do they need our products and services?

Vision and Strategy
What do we need to do?
- Vision—linkage to customer and business requirements
  - What are our mission and goals?
  - What are the most effective ways to achieve the above?
  - What are the major actions required to implement these changes?
- Strategy
  - What are the barriers to implementation?
  - Who will be the process owner and project team?
  - What are the implementation projects, including timing, cost/benefit, and performance expectations?
  - What actions are required to authorize implementation?
  - How will we build momentum for success?

Exhibit 2-12 *(Continued)*

Before starting, be prepared and committed to deliver tangible results
- Do not start until you understand:
  - Why are you reengineering?
  - What are the expected benefits?
  - How does the project relate to other improvement efforts in the business?
- Obtain strong management support for project.
- Select a project team respected by the organization and recognized as thought leaders.
- Focus on the customer and business requirements.
- Deliver tangible results.

Part Two

TRANSACTION PROCESSES

CHAPTER 3

Supply Chain Model for Financial Transaction Environment

3.1   INTRODUCTION

As discussed in chapter 2, the transformation of finance begins with the transaction processes. Transaction processes are the foundation of the finance function:

- Handling all sources and use of funds flow
- Capturing the financial and business information associated with these events

Given that all business events are either a source or use of funds, transaction processes permeate all activities of the business enterprise.

3.2 BENCHMARKING

The transaction processes represent 30 percent to 40 percent of financial operating costs. For most companies, this is a cost of approximately $600,000 to $800,000 per $100 million in revenue.

3.3 REENGINEERING

In this section, we will approach management and reengineering from two perspectives:

1. Business process
2. Operating environment

(a) BUSINESS PROCESS

The major objective of financial reengineering must be to improve business and financial performance. To assure business process requirements are addressed, the book will look at the financial transaction processes from a business process context. The text groups financial transaction into two major business process categories:

Procurement and Value Creation
- Accounts payable
- Payroll
- Time and expense reporting

Revenue Process
- Credit and collections
- Billing
- Accounts receivable

(b) OPERATING ENVIRONMENT

The reinvention of finance is being driven by a fundamental shift in perspective. Transaction operations are now viewed as a business service that must compete with outsource suppliers for financial operations business. This requires a service-driven operation emphasizing the need for a customer-supplier relationship that is based equally on cost and service, i.e., value. This is realistic only when finance's customer has the ultimate decision and control over supplier selection. With these principles as the primary cornerstones of finance's relationship to operations, any efforts short of achieving this customer-driven business model will impede business and financial performance and potentially lead management to outsourcing transaction operations.

3.4 BEST PRACTICES

Best practices can be grouped into two major categories:

- Enabler for business processes to build competitive advantage
- Seamless and transparent operating financial environment that will provide the processing environmental infrastructure for the twenty-first century virtual corporation

Business process best practices include:

- Intervention-free information; timely/real-time recognition of business events
- Recording of information that can provide management with the insights and analytical foundation to build competitive advantage

Operating environment best practices include:

- Control-free transactions emphasizing empowerment and accountability
- Outsourcing and purchasing cards to reduce costs and outsource finance system

3.5 IMPLEMENTATION

Improving business performance and competitive advantage must be the primary reasons for reengineering financial transaction processes. Financial transaction reengineering must deliver tangible improvements to business and financial performance. A results-driven approach will encourage creativity and garner support or transformation of the finance organization.

Reengineering transactions processes can significantly improve business process effectiveness and financial performance:

- Reducing business process and decision cycle times by
  - eliminating bureaucratic procedures and paperwork to authorize spending
  - empowering employees to make business and financial decisions
  - emphasizing employee accountability for the business results that they influence
- Reducing business process cost by
  - outsourcing labor-intensive financial processes
  - improving process integrity by eliminating errors and non-value-added cost
  - creating a "lights out" processing environment requiring no paperwork or manual review and intervention

- eliminating review and validation of all transactions by moving to a process control environment
- Enhancing customer satisfaction by
  - error-free transaction processes
  - ease of doing business
  - capability to operate in a "virtual business process environment"
- Improving management ability to manage operating performance by
  - creating an accessible real-time management information environment
  - developing a business-driven financial transaction data architecture to capture and leverage the information created by each business event that the transaction processes support

(a) OPERATING ENVIRONMENT

The "virtual corporation" is a fundamental transformation of the business enterprise.

It is a fluid organization where employees, vendors, and customers work together in a dynamic real-time environment in which decisions, commitments, and actions among all parties occur simultaneously.

The virtual corporate operating principles closely resemble the principle of Chaos Theory. Fundamental changes to the financial transaction and control environment are required to accommodate this emerging business environment. A virtual corporation requires a virtual finance organization and financial processes.

The virtual corporation is an extension of supply-chain management. During the 1990s, supply-chain management has been a major part of business process reengineering in many companies.

Supply-chain management emphasizes coordinating the activities of employees, vendors, and customers to improve the value of products and services and, in turn, to increase customer satisfaction and profitability.

The next improvement has been a shift in emphasis from coordination or management to integrating the supply chain. A major design characteristic of an integrated process is the elimination of the boundaries between vendors, employees, and customers. An integrated business process is intrinsically a "virtual" process. Ergo the "virtual corporation"—a natural evolution in supply-chain management and the definition for the twenty-first century corporation.

The expected improvements to product and service capabilities and value resulting from an integrated, or virtual, supply chain include:

- Reducing or eliminating cycle times between customer and supplier activities
- Creating a closer relationship with customers to maximize the value of the products and services by
  - understanding customers' business and competitive position
  - anticipating product and service requirements
- Building a partnership based on trust where customer and vendor see that their success is dependent on each other
  - encouraging a creative and dynamic environment that quickly adapts to change
  - empowering business process teams to make commitments immediately with absolute confidence that the associated actions will be followed through expeditiously without further approvals

Financial transaction processes are the underlying business administrative infrastructure of the supply chain. Financial transactions occur at every major step of the supply chain.

3.5 Implementation

The transaction operating environment will be central to creating the virtual corporation. The goal for reengineering financial processes is to build competitive advantage. With the virtual corporation becoming the paradigm for the twenty-first century corporation, financial process reengineering must achieve a financial process and control environment supporting a virtual corporation.

The virtual corporation is a dynamic real-time environment where:

- Customer and vendor business processes are seamless.
- Financial transaction processes are transparent and occur simultaneously with each business event.
- Financial controls allow business decisions and events to occur unimpeded in an "apparently" control-free environment.

Financial transaction processes begin with the recognition of a business event that will result in a financial settlement. All business events are based on an explicit or implied agreement to compensate a company or individual for the services or products provided.

The major business events of the supply chain process are:

- *Procure:* vendors selling services and products
- *Create:* employees and vendors providing services to create products and services for the company
- *Provide:* the company, in turn, using these products and services to fulfill its customers' requirements

All of these events share a set of common characteristics. For example, one company's revenue process is part of another company's procurement process—these processes are mirror images of each other. They are not only similar, but also occur simultaneously in each company, as reflected by the descriptions above.

Employees providing their services for their employer are generally associated with a service or product that their employer is providing to the customer, and, in turn, the customer follows suit. A revenue and expense neutral definition for financial transaction processes has significant implications for reengineering strategies for the transaction processes. A revenue and expense neutral approach to reengineering the financial processes is the first major step toward creating the financial process model for the virtual corporation.

Financial transaction reengineering is the "yellow brick road" to the virtual corporation. Chapter 4 in this section lays out the model and strategies to repeating the virtual financial transaction environment. Finance has the opportunity to create not only a real-time infrastructure to support the virtual corporation, but also the management paradigms and process vision that will provide the bridge to the twenty-first century corporation—the virtual corporation.

3.6   REENGINEERED PROCESS FLOW

The financial model for the virtual corporation was first introduced in chapter 1, exhibit 1-2. Exhibit 3-1 expands this model to reflect the requirements for finance to operate information and transaction processes and infrastructure that will be the foundation for the virtual corporation.

3.7   MEASURING PERFORMANCE

The best measure of financial transaction performance is the transparent or invisible approval and processing of a transaction. A transparent process requires the elimination of errors and bureaucracy and results de facto in a low-cost and virtual process.

Exhibit 3-1 Virtual Finance Operating Model

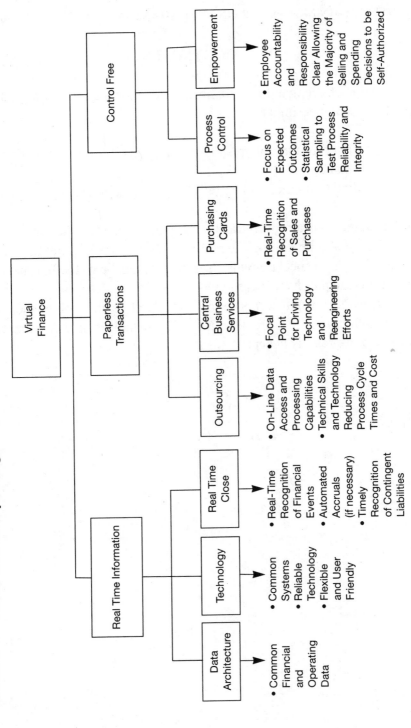

3.8   KEY CHALLENGES

The major challenges to realizing the full potential from transaction process reengineering are:

- Delivering tangible results that improve business process performance
- Creating momentum by building on early successes

Once finance has a proven track record, the subject of the virtual corporation should be raised. The reality of the virtual corporation can be seen every day, especially with the rapid expansion of the Internet and the corporate purchasing card.

Once the virtual corporation is received as inevitable, then the recommendations that are set out for the virtual finance organization will be more readily accepted.

CHAPTER 4

Accounts Payable and the Procurement Process

4.1 INTRODUCTION

Accounts payable process and bureaucracy are synonymous. Documentation and multiple approvals, combined with the volume of daily purchases, have made accounts payable one of the highest cost areas in finance.

From a traditional functional or departmental perspective, the primary responsibilities of accounts payable include:

- Accounting for the receipt of goods and services
- Classifying expenditures in accordance with company policy and generally accepted accounting principles (GAAP)
- Authorizing vendor payment

From a business process perspective, transaction processes are the administrative infrastructure and utilities of the business enterprise. All business events or activities that have a financial impact will be recognized and tracked by one or more of the transaction processes.

Another way of looking at this is that transaction processes provide the economic stimulus and business information that both triggers and tracks each business event and business process cycle. Combining the concepts of business process life cycle with a financial and administration utility begins to provide some insight as to how financial transaction processes and business process life cycles are in sync and interdependent:

Financial Transaction	*Business Process*
Financial Generation	Business events that generate the sources of funds for core business processes
Financial Distribution	Funds and related business information grid that wires and integrates business processes across the business enterprise
Financial Service	Access funds and business information triggering business event that utilizes financial resources to create economic value

Looking at transaction processes as a financial utility is a critical paradigm shift required for finance to support the creation of the virtual corporation. As long as financial intervention is required at the time of a business event, business processes will continue to be discrete activities, with finance serving as a gatekeeper at each step of the process. Eliminating finance's gatekeeper role will require a financial control and process environment that does not require physical or tangible evidence at the time of the business event.

Businesses cannot run without relying upon electric and telephone utilities. We pick up a phone or turn on a light without any doubt that the service will be available for use. We rely upon these utilities throughout the day, confident that:

- Service (funding and business information) will be available on demand.
- Service charges and related information will be accumulated and reported on a periodic basis without authorization or intervention at the time service is provided.

By approaching transaction processes from the perspective of a financial utility, we can begin to see that:

- Financial transactions are the lifeblood of the business enterprise.
- Tangible evidence that the transaction processes are being effectively managed is not required because confidence in process reliability and availability are taken for granted.

4.2 BENCHMARKING

(a) AVERAGE

Accounts payable is one of the highest cost areas in finance. On average, accounts payable represents 10 percent of the total cost of finance, with spending typically ranging from .1 percent to .2 percent of revenues. This translates into a cost of between $100,000 and $200,000 for a $100 million company and between $1 million and $2 million for a $1 billion company. When the costs of processing approvals, matching documents, creating purchase orders, and following up on errors or problems are taken into account, the total cost to the organization could be five times this amount, resulting in a total process cost of between 1 percent and 2 percent of revenues, or $1 million to $2 million for a $100 million company.

Another way to measure accounts payable cost is to take the total number of invoices processed against the total departmental cost of accounts payable. The average company will process invoices in the range of $3 to $7 an invoice, though I have seen this number exceed $10 per invoice. The cost of creating a purchase order ranges from $150 to $225 in most companies.

(b) WORLD CLASS

The process reengineering described in the following sections allows companies to reduce their accounts payable costs by between 50 percent and 75 percent. This can represent savings of $50,000 to $150,000 for a $100 million company and $500,000 to $1.5 million for a $1 billion company. These savings do not reflect the savings that would be realized in the procurement process.

4.3 REENGINEERING

The negative image of the accounts payable process has relegated much of accounts payable reengineering to a cost-reduction effort. However, the business information accessible through this process could provide management with insight that could lead to improved financial and business performance.

Accounts payable is the major source of financial data. All non-payroll expenditures are handled by the accounts payable process. Except for amortization/depreciation and payroll, all business process cost and capital spending is recorded through the accounts payable process. With purchase goods and services representing approximately 60 percent to 70 percent of a company's operating cost, the accounts payable process offers a tremendous opportunity for finance to create an information-rich financial and business information environment.

Accounts payable pervasiveness throughout all business processes offers finance an opportunity to reduce cost and improve business process effectiveness.

The primary cost drivers of accounts payable are paper handling and transaction volume. The paper-intensive process has resulted in labor cost typically representing 60 percent to 70 percent of the cost in accounts payable.

High cost and high frustration with antiquated bureaucratic procedures require that process cost and efficiency be the top priorities. To accomplish a dramatic reduction in cost and the elimination of bureaucracy, a reengineered accounts payable process will have to achieve the following goals:

- Paperless processing
- Self-authorized purchasing
- Spending controls focused on managing process integrity through spending budgets and forecasting
- Elimination of duplication of work by reengineering accounts payable in conjunction with the procurement process

In addition to accomplishing the above, a world-class accounts payable process will have the following attributes:

- Easy and timely access to financial and operating data
- Leveraging financial and business systems integration by establishing a common definition of purchasing information
- Data structure for financial and operating systems

4.4   BEST PRACTICES

Consolidation, outsourcing, and elimination are the primary focus of accounts payable best practices. The ideal best practice is a process environment where the accounts payable process is transparent or invisible.

The following best practices offer reengineering solutions that can lead to the ideal process state:

- Eliminate purchase orders except for annual purchase agreements.
- Eliminate invoices by relying on annual purchase agreements to pay on:
  - receipt
  - consumption
- Implement purchasing card program for 90-percent-plus purchase transactions.
- Consolidate vendor payments across supplier divisions and company's own divisions and operating locations.
- Eliminate checks by shifting to electronic funds transfer.
- Implement electronic data interchange for capturing all transaction information.
- Outsource accounts payable processing to shared services of financial outsourcing vendor.
- Eliminate duplicate processing, handling, and retention of transaction records.
- Establish common vendor codes for all division and financial and operating systems.

4.5   IMPLEMENTATION

As discussed above, transaction process reengineering should be done in conjunction with the business processes it supports. Consequently, this book looks first at accounts payable in terms of improving the effectiveness of the procurement process.

The book then reviews two major reengineering initiatives that are required to create a world-class accounts payable process:

1. Outsourcing accounts payable to third-party vendors or shared services
2. Implementing purchasing card programs for 90-percent-plus of purchasing transactions

(a)   PROCUREMENT PROCESS

The procurement process major goals include:

- Selecting the right suppliers of products and services to build competitive advantage
- Coordinating the ordering of products and services to meet business needs while minimizing cost
- Managing and evaluating vendor performance to assure that vendors and their products and services are meeting current and future business requirements

(i)   Financial Utility Requirements

Utilizing the financial utility concept, the book will look at accounts payable from the following perspective:

- *Supplier selection:*   Financial generation of sources and uses of funds
- *Coordinating purchases:*   Financial distribution of financial and business information relied upon to manage business results
- *Managing and evaluating suppliers:*   Financial services assessing the contribution of the supplier to creating economic value for the business enterprise

From this perspective, the goals of the accounts payable process will be the following:

Supplier Selection: Financial Generation. The major objective of the accounts payable process is to assure that all relevant financial and business information is recorded at the time of the sourcing decision. This serves two major purposes:

1. Impact on sources and uses of funds is known. Assuring that the financial implications of decision are known on a real-time basis eliminates the need for approvals at the time of an individual purchase decision.
2. Uninterrupted access to financial information and preauthorization allows financial and business decisions to occur in a real-time, or virtual, environment.

The above allows us to meet the criteria for "financial generation": assuring that financial resources—power—are available on demand.

Coordinating Purchases: Financial Distribution. In this stage, the major responsibility of the accounts payable process is to assure that the necessary information is accessible throughout the business enterprise. By providing an integrated financial and management information environment, finance can distribute relevant financial and procurement information to enable management to plan and manage resource requirements.

This process step is aimed at providing information to plan and make decisions.

Managing Suppliers: Financial Services. The major goal of this stage is the transformation of business knowledge (supplier management) with financial resources (financial services) to create economic wealth. This is the action stage of both the financial utility and procurement processes. The previous two stages were aimed at planning and providing the technology and administrative infrastructure to enable Stage 3 to occur—creation of economic value and, in turn, shareholder wealth.

4.5 Implementation

In this stage, the major objective for the accounts payable process must be to capture the appropriate information to allow management to manage results and to assess suppliers' performance against business needs and contractual obligations.

(ii) Procurement Process Reengineering

Before undertaking reengineering of the procurement process, finance must define a clear vision of the role of financial control and management accountability for all financial transactions.

The financial utility control paradigm that we are striving toward is a "control-free transaction environment." For accounts payable, a control-free environment will be achieved by eliminating:

* Bureaucracy
* Hierarchical control and approvals
* Paperwork

By eliminating the control paradigms, finance is now in a position to challenge management's control paradigms. A proactive approach to creating a virtual control environment will eliminate finance as a convenient scapegoat for ineffective and bureaucratic administrative procedures that have been created by purchasing organization.

To further simplify the financial control considerations, controls should be driven by the business context and financial risk. Two major factors can help differentiate control requirements:

1. Defining the scope or boundaries where the procurement process can significantly add value.
   * The major goals for the procurement process stated above are appropriate for production purchases or purchases of products and services critical to the core competencies of the business enterprise. Reengineering should focus on how the procurement process can build competitive advantage.

- However, the majority of transactions are for small-value nonproduction and noncore purchases. Any purchasing involvement in these buys, with the exception of national contracts for items like office supplies, will impede buy decisions and generally result in the cost of the purchasing activities exceeding the cost of the products and services acquired. Consequently, for small purchases the goal of procurement process reengineering is to eliminate all interventions and controls.
- Emphasizing the cost of purchasing intervention on small purchases is essential to successfully leveraging the benefits of purchasing cards. If any intervention occurs, the majority of the anticipated saving will be eliminated. The potential for checking will result in documentation, and justification of purchases will be documented—even if policy states that documentation is not required. Employees concerned that they will be second-guessed will out of political necessity have sufficient support to justify their actions.
- The control-free environment envisioned by the financial utility relies upon financial performance against forecast and budgets as a tool to assess control compliance. Internal controls shift from process compliance to expected outcomes. If transaction controls are effective, then finance will expect specific financial results or outcomes. If these results are inconsistent with forecast or operational and financial relationships, then a red flag will trigger evaluation of financial activity.
- We will expand on this control environment in chapter 11.
2. Determining who should have control over purchasing decisions.
   - Accountability and responsibility alignment requires that purchasing decisions be made by the individual or team

that will be using the vendors' products and services. This suggests that the purchasing process is a support process rather than a process that dictates to the organization. Empowerment combined with the alignment of responsibility and accountability are key elements of the financial utility and, in turn, the virtual corporation.

(b) SUPPLIER SELECTION

A major theme that crosses all steps of the procurement process is a constant emphasis on leveraging suppliers' products and services to build competitive advantage. This requires a shift in focus from policies and procedures to delivering tangible results.

A transition to a results-driven process requires that policies emphasize the character and attributes that represent process integrity rather than dictating activities and delineating hierarchical responsibilities. This topic is covered thoroughly in chapter 11, Internal Audit.

Therefore, the internal control environment focuses on meeting commitments or expected financial and business outcomes. While a code of conduct and ethics is essential to managing in a control-free environment, these policies emphasize management accountability and good faith to act in the best interests of the company.

It will be difficult to maintain a results-driven process relying upon management's good faith if management's decisions are constantly reviewed and authorized. An environment emphasizing management review and authorization leads to an environment that:

- Implies that employees cannot be trusted; and
- Allows employees plausible deniability because accountability is ambiguous.

In other words, the financial utility "control-free environment" is required to develop a world-class procurement process. Eliminating all vestiges of distrust and deniability is essential to focusing attention on delivering results. By eliminating all the policies and procedures that encourage the procurement and financial organization, the only thing left for procurement and finance is to improve business and financial results.

The supplier-selection process is a trigger point to shifting the emphasis of the procurement process to leveraging suppliers' products and services to build competitive advantage. Supplier selection is at the very beginning of the procurement process. The tone set during this effort will dictate the tone carried throughout the process.

The first step to making this change is turning to the strategic side of procurement that supports development, capital investment planning, and the annual operating plan and budgeting activity.

Accounts payable can reinforce and support the change in focus by:

- Providing performance information on existing suppliers
- Emphasizing supplier performance criteria and commitments as a major component of establishing the supplier accounts payable file

Establishing and maintaining performance-oriented supplier files will draw attention to what performance measurements and evaluation criteria are necessary to support the supplier management process, thereby assuring that these new criteria can be directly integrated into the supplier management activity. More importantly, providing real-time access to supplier performance criteria and pricing and ordering terms allows the remainder of the procurement process to rely upon these files for planning, ordering, and evaluating supplier performance.

This step is the foundation for creating a virtual payables and procurement process. Sufficient effort is made at the time of the supplier selection to establish pricing and performance expectations to eliminate the need to question or check pricing and performance criteria. The remaining steps in the process then deal with managing supplier activity to achieve performance expectations or to find new suppliers that can.

(c) RESOURCE REQUIREMENTS PLANNING

Resource requirements planning requires an understanding of:

- Current-period resource or inventory position
- Future-period resource requirements
- Lead time, reliability, and availability of required resources for production scheduling

In general, we associate resource requirements planning with near-term production planning and scheduling. Yet this same methodology applies to the annual capacity planning component of the supplier selection process.

In the supplier selection process, accounts payable's primary responsibilities are transmitting historical performance and setting up supplier files that will be relied upon for the remaining steps of the procurement process. In the resource planning process, accounts payable can become an important source of financial and operating information to improve the effectiveness of resource planning.

The potential value of information available through accounts payable is most apparent in the resource planning process. The level of detail and quality of accounts payable information will be a major determinant of the effectiveness of the resource planning process. Historically, accounts payable detail for financial reporting purposes has been reported in aggregate by the appropriate general-ledger account.

At the general-ledger level, the traditional source for financial reporting, company and product detail are not recorded. This becomes a problem where the general-ledger system is not integrated with the accounts payable system. In this environment, access to accounts payable detail is generally not accessible for financial reporting and analysis. Further, in most cases, the accounts payable system will record the vendor name but not the detail of products and services purchased—providing better but still limited information that is of value for operating management.

This encourages, if not demands, that management rely on purchasing, inventory, and manufacturing systems to plan and manage operations. These systems were developed, in part, to compensate for the limited value of financial reporting. Developing systems to compensate for poor financial systems is no longer a viable long-term option. The financial systems environment must be the enabler for creating an integrated management information environment (see chapter 8).

Stand-alone operating systems increase costs and cloud management accountability. The ramifications of this systems environment include:

- Higher administrative costs resulting from duplicate processing of data
- Higher maintenance and development costs from supporting two systems that rely on the same data source rather than one system supporting all reporting requirements
- Incompatible financial and operating data providing management with a shield to dispute financial results as not accurately reflecting business results

This allows operating management to place a disclaimer on financial reporting. With operating reports that do not tie to financial reports, operating managers emphasize that they rely on the operating systems to plan and manage the business. When financials do not readily tie to operating forecast and results for the same time periods, management will argue that financial reports are irrelevant to managing business results.

To eliminate the costs and disclaimers, finance must move to a common database for both operating and financial reporting. The procurement process owners must have accountability for maintaining the integrity of purchasing information. From a financial accounting perspective, finance only needs total current period purchases as an aggregated level that is directly associated with accounting terms used for external reporting. In other words, the number of accounting classifications that purchases will be classified under will be as few as a dozen accounts for all purchases—not hundreds of accounting classifications.

The goal of the accounts payable process for information reporting is to unshackle accounts payable information from the general ledger's "chart of accounts." By limiting financial accounting classifications for payables, we are breaking the dependence of the chart of accounts to provide the reporting structure for management reporting.

Unable to rely on the chart of accounts for classifying purchasing information, finance will be required to rely on the source data for ad hoc and management reporting. By simplifying the accounting classifications, this system minimizes financial accounting requirements from the accounts payable process. This minimalist financial accounting classification strategy will allow finance to move toward common systems, or at least common databases, for both financial and operating management.

By eliminating the financial accounting data requirements from accounts payable, finance can then turn to management and ask what its information and system support requirements are. Since financial accounting requirements are at such a high level, financial accounting reporting could eliminate the majority of information and detail normally inputted into the accounts payable system. Taking the approach that finance will only provide information and support that is required by management, combined with the fact that finance will no longer need the majority of the information currently available, we are hoping to trigger management to define their information needs.

Pointing out that financial systems in the future will be driven by operating management requirements, with little required for external reporting purposes, finance can advocate the migration of accounts payable data and reporting to a common system. This system could be a manufacturing or financial application. The major factor determining which application is selected will be management requirements. From a financial accounting standpoint, finance can tap into the appropriate databases to gather the necessary information for external reporting. In other words, financial accounting information requirements are so minimal that there is no need for the data to be reported by a financial application.

The information and system support requirements for accounts payable will then be determined in large part by the requirements of the procurement process. The book will address these information needs by the major procurement process steps. For resource planning purposes, the major information requirements are:

- Vendor sourcing information
  - vendors and related products and service offerings
  - pricing, quality, reliability, and availability of resources by vendor
  - vendor contact
  - lead times
  - purchasing constraints or limitations related to buy quantities or other relevant factors
- Pipeline information
  - incoming resources
  - resources on hand

- resources in transit to both company-owned locations and customers
- access to external systems for identifying new products and new sources for existing products

(d)   SUPPLIER MANAGEMENT

There are two major aspects of the supplier management process:

1. Tracking and evaluating supplier performance
2. Taking appropriate actions based on supplier results

The tracking metrics are identified and set up during the supplier selection process. The accounts payable process automatically captures all the metric data that is used for performance reporting.

(e)   PURCHASING CARD PROGRAMS

Implementing purchasing card programs is the leading best practice for accounts payable. It is aimed at eliminating the bureaucracy and the majority of the cost incurred for processing accounts payable by using credit cards, with no preapproval requirements. This requires changes to the internal controls to allow for self-authorization and emphasizing spending control against budget and forecasted spending.

With low-dollar transactions typically representing 80 percent of the cost of accounts payable, while equaling only about 20 percent of total purchases, cost-saving potential is enormous, and the financial exposure is manageable.

The following list highlights the operating and business practices of a purchasing card program:

- Single, consolidated payment for all credit card purchases
- Credit card statements serve as validation and authorization of purchases
- Programs are migrating to a short list of national vendors providing companies access to new suppliers and potential for leveraging the purchasing power of others participating in the credit card program
- Number of days sales outstanding for the supplier is significantly reduced and in most cases also reducing their billing cost (see chapter 7)
- An electronic database file of all credit card transactions is transmitted monthly, with the goal of allowing daily access to credit card transactions
- Department and accounting codes can be designed into the credit card allowing the electronic data files to
  - directly post entries to the general ledger
  - establish project accounts, a capital program, or special projects

Efforts by credit card vendors to enhance and standardize transaction data offer the potential for capturing valuable business and financial data that is not currently available to most companies due to the limitations of their accounts payable applications and overall systems environment.

Because cards are assigned to individuals—not departments—cardholders are self-authorizing transactions; therefore, no one can pass responsibility to a third party for spending that violates company policy. The reality is that credit card programs are enhancing internal controls over spending.

In addition, a major outgrowth of the purchasing card program is focusing management's attention on the procurement process. Credit card program implementation requires identifying which vendors to target for using the purchasing card. The primary factors used to separate vendors are dollar value and the strategic importance of the supplier to the success of a company's business.

This is leading companies to establish a two-tier supplier structure and management program. The goal of the purchasing card program is not only to reduce the costs associated with purchases, but also to eliminate the purchasing oversight and administrative costs for the second-tier suppliers. Concentrating on strategic suppliers, purchasing can increase its efforts on supplier management and performance.

(f)   SHARED SERVICE: CENTRALIZING ACCOUNTS PAYABLE

The primary reasons that companies have been centralizing accounts payable are to reduce:

- Management costs by increasing spans of control
- Systems costs by consolidating systems and applications
- Labor, facilities, and overhead costs by moving to a low-wage and low–cost-of-living location

These benefits can result in savings of 25 percent to 40 percent of current accounts payable cost. A centralization effort provides management with a focal point to maintain attention and pressure on the speed of implementation.

A centralization strategy also is aimed at leveraging best practices, such as purchasing card programs. With management responsible for all accounts payable activities across a company, implementing a best practice at a centralized shared service center will result in the simultaneous implementation of this practice across the company.

This could reduce the time of implementing best practices across a company by months, and, for large companies, years.

(g) TECHNOLOGICAL SOLUTIONS

Technological solutions have historically been the predominant focus of most finance productivity efforts. Although reengineering has been enjoying great success, financial organizations continue to be lured to high-tech solutions—but with limited results. Two areas receiving the most attention over the past few years have been automated matching of purchasing orders, invoices, and receivers (often called automatch), and financial electronic data interchange (EDI).

Although automatch had the appeal of eliminating paper shuffling and duplication of work, experience with automatch has demonstrated that the benefits do not exist. On average, more than 15 percent of invoices do not match against the authorizing purchase orders. This leads to high-cost intervention and lengthening of cycle times, as well as straining vendor relations in an era when strategic alliances and business partnerships are more critical to building competitive advantage than the cost of accounts payable.

Reengineering solutions, on the other hand, have focused on eliminating the matching process, which in turn eliminates the need for automatch. Similarly, the practical benefits of EDI are elusive. Companies are struggling with EDI for initiating purchase orders. Every buyer wants to order by EDI, but most buyers do not have the clout to demand that the vendors do business with them through EDI. The most notable exceptions are in industries in which the customer has a dominant position over a vendor, allowing the customer to dictate the terms of doing business. This is the case with the automotive industry and in distribution businesses with high transaction volumes and a high number of stockkeeping units or products.

In summary, technology is a Pandora's box for the accounts payable process. Using technology to eliminate manual process has the effect of embedding high-cost business practices into the fabric of a company. While management believes that cost savings have been achieved by reducing manual processing, the hidden cost of procurement goes unnoticed. The purchasing process could represent as much as five to ten times the accounts payable cost for a purchase. This hidden savings is a major reason for pursuing procurement process reengineering in conjunction with the accounts payable process.

4.6 REENGINEERED PROCESS FLOW

An example of a reengineered process flow is shown in exhibit 4-1. The accounts payable process in the exhibit starts with either a procurement card purchase or the issuance of a purchase order. The credit card company's monthly statement or the vendor's bill is manually entered in the system. Cost centers are automatically identified because each employee has his or her own account number. Once information is entered, the system updates the general-ledger accounts payable system and issues a check or electronic funds transfer (EFT) payment. Once information is entered in the system, it is also available on-line.

4.7 MEASURING PERFORMANCE

Exhibit 4-2 can be used to assess current and future performance. It can be used at various points throughout the reengineering process to track progress. These measures are also valuable for focusing the reengineering teams' efforts on improvements that will deliver tangible results.

Following is the reengineering direction that should be taken as a result of using these measures to improve process performance.

1. *Cost drivers.* Transaction volume and errors are the biggest drivers of cost. Minimize process complexity to reduce error rates and increase use of purchasing cards to reduce transaction volumes.

Exhibit 4-1 Accounts Payable Process Flow

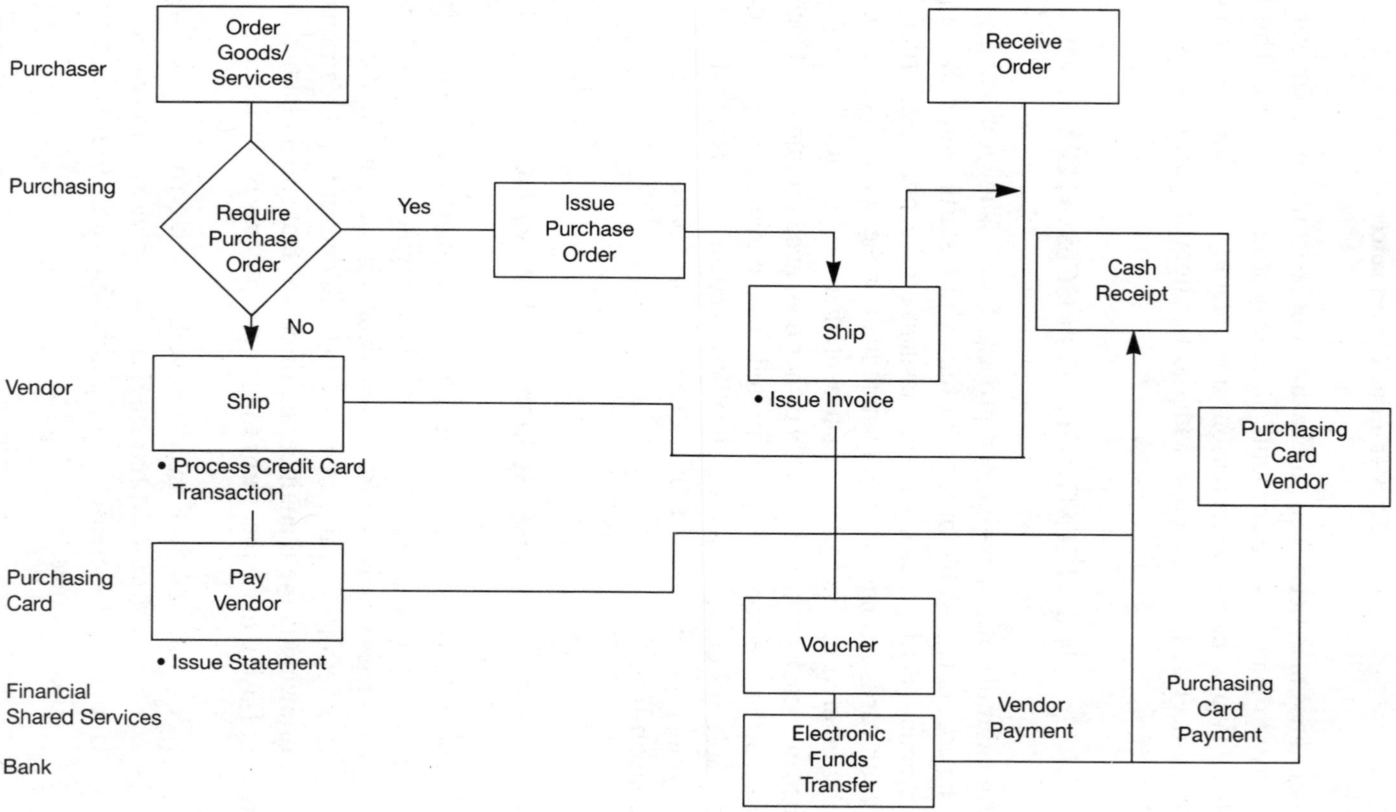

Purchaser

Purchasing

Vendor

Purchasing Card

Financial Shared Services

Bank

Order Goods/Services

Require Purchase Order — Yes → Issue Purchase Order

No

Ship
• Process Credit Card Transaction

Ship
• Issue Invoice

Receive Order

Cash Receipt

Purchasing Card Vendor

Pay Vendor
• Issue Statement

Voucher

Electronic Funds Transfer

Vendor Payment

Purchasing Card Payment

Exhibit 4-2 Performance Measures

Quality/Service	Cost Drivers
Elimination of invoices	Number of line items
Number of invoices not posted in day of receipt	Number of invoices
	Number of active vendors
Number of invoices and purchase orders matched first time	Percent invoices with prior POs
	Number of checks issued
Payment on receipt	Number of authorizations required
Percentage of self-authorized transactions (i.e., purchasing cards)	Records retention requirements

Productivity Measures

Invoices/check

Productivity

Number of checks
Number of checks/invoices
Number of invoices/purchase orders
Checks/supplier per month
Number of invoices/suppliers

Dollar value of invoice
Number of invoices/number of checks

Quality Measures

Cycle time—process
Percent errors/defect
Percent cash discounts taken

2. *Productivity measure.* Reducing invoice processing volume is the best indicator of improved productivity. Productivity can be influenced by streamlining processes or eliminating the activity. The best choice is activity elimination.

3. *Quality process.* Quality of the process is best measured by the transparency of processing the transaction.

As discussed in the reengineering section, some questions to keep in mind when tracking and measuring performance are:

- Is there easy, timely access to information?
- Has control of spending been delegated to the appropriate area of responsibility?
- Is there same-day recognition of liability?
- Is the process paperless or nearly so?

- Has a plan been put in place to migrate to a single payable system and processing center?
- Have internal controls been redesigned to focus on managing the spending process and not the transaction?
- What integration with financial systems such as the general ledger has occurred?
- Have financial and business information requirements been identified?
- Is there an enterprise-wide initiative to establish common systems and common data architecture?

4.8   KEY CHALLENGES

The key challenges that the finance manager will face in implementing a change agenda for accounts payable are:

- Finance's cultural environment may lead to resistance to the concept of purchasing cards.
- Dedicated resources for implementation will prove to be elusive. The tendency is to see this type of effort being coordinated in conjunction with the ongoing activities in the accounts payable department.
- A short time frame is essential to demonstrating success and building momentum for change. However, management's general frustration with the accounts payable process leads people to believe that reengineering will require a long-term effort.

Accounts payable reengineering offers finance an opportunity to deliver significant cost savings across the business and improve purchasing and decision cycle times. Accounts payable provides finance with a focal point for shifting the emphasis on systems from transaction processing to information management. The value of capturing accounts payable data is the information that can be used to analyze cost and improve business performance.

Reengineering the accounts payable process must be one of the highest priority reengineering initiatives. The cost savings are significant. The reduction in management's frustration with financial controls and bureaucracy is tangible. The emphasis on eliminating transaction processing and focusing on procurement process will improve the competitiveness of your company.

Further, the focus on elimination of activities controls and shifting to a simple purchasing process will allow for a faster implementation process than normally would be expected.

The dilemma for finance is whether to:

- Wait until management is prepared to reengineer the procurement process; or
- Use accounts payable reengineering as the trigger to reengineering the procurement process.

Finance is not in a position to wait. The bureaucracy and cost of the accounts payable process is so pervasive across the business enterprise that it will prevent the transformation of the business enterprise to the twenty-first century virtual corporation. Industry leadership in the twenty-first century will be determined in large part by who are the first to achieve a virtual corporate environment.

A real-time information environment, effective and focused business processes, and employees empowered to take action are among the major attributes of the virtual corporation. A company that achieves a virtual business process environment will be in a competitive position to respond and meet customer requirements much faster than its competitors. Over time, this will lead to the virtual corporation capturing market share and increasing profitability at the expense of those who have not made the transition.

Change agent is a major attribute of the leadership team of a world-class finance organization. An advocacy role for finance is necessary in order to accomplish its primary mission—to create share-holder wealth. If wealth creation is dependent on improving business process performance, then finance must take the actions necessary to trigger business management to undertake a business process reengineering effort.

We can try to facilitate change by:

- Advocating change through words and reports; or
- Taking an aggressive approach to financial reengineering that will lead to addressing business process issues that intersect and impact financial processes.

Management complacency is the typical reaction to words and reports. Complacency will result in maintaining the status quo and allowing organizational inertia to hinder change.

An aggressive approach will be necessary in an environment where there is little business process reengineering experience or interest. An aggressive approach requires a win-win strategy. A win-win strategy requires a carrot-and-stick approach:

- *Carrot:* Reducing cost and bureaucracy
- *Stick:* Recommending specific changes to business processes that will allow us to get the carrot

CHAPTER 5

Payroll

5.1 INTRODUCTION

The payroll process is the one financial process that touches every employee, and in a very personal way. Compensation, taxes, and deductions—medical and benefit plans, savings plans, stock purchase plans, retirement accounts—all are processed and recorded on the employee's payroll statement.

This is a complex process that gets only more difficult as a result of constant changes, including:

- Employee status—promotions, transfers, annual increases, new hires
- State, local, and federal tax laws
- Deductions for new benefit plans or adjustments to existing plans

5.2 BENCHMARKING

Payroll costs average only .08 percent of revenues, or $80,000 for $100 million in sales, but the cost that can be most readily identified with is the cost per check, which averages $4–$6. While cost per transaction does not appear excessively high, payroll has been one of the first financial operations to be outsourced. This outsourcing has been driven by not only the cost of payroll operations, but also the headaches associated with tax filing, compliance, and issuance of W-2 forms.

Outsourcing combined with the best practices discussed in this chapter can lead to savings of 25 percent to 50 percent of current payroll cost. This could result in savings of $20,000 to $40,000 for a $100 million company and $200,000 to $400,000 for a $1 billion company.

5.3 REENGINEERING

Today, the payroll outsourcing business is growing at a double-digit rate. These companies not only process payroll and related employee taxes, but also are beginning to expand into selling and managing employee benefit plans.

The trend to offering benefits is consistent with the scope of the payroll process. Payroll is part of the employee, or human resources performance, process. Many companies have the payroll function report to human resources. Payroll systems are now being integrated with the human resources systems, which is consistent with the trend toward business process management.

Employee performance is critical to a company's success. What companies are realizing is that outsourcing does not mean losing control. In fact, outsourcing provides most businesses with better technology and processing capabilities. So, human resources can focus on employee performance instead of managing financial systems and a highly complex and high-risk financial activity.

Payroll, however, is a major component of a company's product and service cost. The quality and accessibility to labor cost are essential to supporting a world-class cost and performance management process. Because payroll can provide management with better information to manage business performance, outsourcing alone will not provide you with a world-class payroll process.

Reengineering payroll must address two issues:

1. Minimizing the cost of payroll processing
2. Maximizing the value of payroll information

As is the case with all transaction processes, intervention is the primary driver of transaction processing cost. The implication for payroll is that outsourcing will reduce the general cost of processing. But to maximize cost savings, developing a "control-free environment" will be required.

A control-free environment relies upon self-authorization and process integrity measured against expected outcomes. In other words, a certain employment level combined with standard shifts and standardized pay grades can allow management to evaluate the validity of labor cost without checking time cards. Therefore, the only employee intervention expected would be for exceptions such as vacation, sick time, and overtime. Employee intervention will be expected for these items and be self-authorized.

Another driver of payroll costs is the number of stand-alone payroll systems and benefit plans. Consolidating systems can be accomplished through outsourcing. Consolidation of benefit plans, though a cost driver for payroll, must be considered from a business viewpoint. Labor agreements and disparity in cost of living across operating locations are often the major factors leading to multiple benefit plans. However, management should incur and fully recognize the added administrative cost resulting from a proliferation of benefit plans.

5.4 BEST PRACTICES

The major factor holding back a more aggressive trend to outsourcing is that payroll costs are relatively low in most companies. This is due to aggressive centralization and the uniqueness of payroll practices and benefits. This often forces outsource vendors to customize their products, which increases their cost structure and ability to demonstrate a strong cost advantage.

Due to the cost advantage of centralized payroll operations, the first step in reengineering is centralization. After centralization, which then becomes cost-competitive with outsourcing, there are opportunities for improvement within the practices associated with payroll data collection and processing. These include:

- Having a high percentage of employees use direct deposit as method of receiving their paychecks
- Reimbursing business expenses through paychecks (no separate drafts issued)
- Economizing on payroll processing through shared services
- Minimizing payroll cycles
- Establishing common policies, systems, and processes for payroll administration across the organization
- Instituting common benefit programs
- Integrating payroll and human resource systems
- Outsourcing payroll processing and administration
- Having exception-based payroll reporting for hourly employees
  - automatic payroll processing based upon standard hours and vacation schedules

- changes in hours (sick time, vacation days, overtime) reported on exception basis

5.5 IMPLEMENTATION

The number of employees and the number of disbursements are the major cost drivers of payroll cost. Given that corporate restructuring most likely will not be triggered by a payroll reengineering assignment, we will assume that the payroll department will have little control over the number of employees. Reducing the number of payroll disbursements is an option, but typically not one pursued. The opportunities are nevertheless significant. If a company is on a weekly payroll that is shifted to a biweekly payroll, it can expect to save 25 percent to 50 percent of costs by reducing the activity level by 50 percent.

The number of unique payroll cycles offers a more manageable opportunity. Typically, companies have three payroll cycles: weekly, biweekly, and monthly. These unique cycles must be maintained and supported independently, which leads to duplication of effort and often duplicate systems. By reducing the number of payroll cycles, a company saves by reducing activity levels, and minimizing staffing levels to nonpeak period requirements. In short, with multiple payroll cycles, payroll is in a constant peak environment requiring excessive resource demands.

In addition to payroll cycles and disbursements, the collection procedure can be a source of extensive processing. Many manufacturing-based companies or service companies with high levels of hourly employees require collection and processing of time cards. This requires that local operations manage paper processing, which must be entered into the corporate payroll system. This extensive paper-processing trail has led many companies to pursue automated time-keeping—computer time cards and collection. While this reduces handling costs, it still requires investment and spending to support and maintain the system. Computer time collection is an improvement over paper but not enough to justify the investment in payroll processing costs alone. If payroll processing cost is the prime driver, the goal should be to eliminate payroll processing steps. If this is the case, the objective should be to report payroll hours on an exception basis and minimize the processing associated with timekeeping for sick days, holidays, and vacations.

However, if a company is pursuing activity-based management or is closely monitoring labor cost on a manufacturing department basis, then computer timekeeping may be merited by the anticipated cost-saving achieved by improved management information.

There are three major technology areas to be considered:

1. Installing and using outsourcing vendors' computer applications
2. Integrating payroll systems with the human resource systems
3. Supporting cost management systems and applications for activity costing and project cost management

5.6 REENGINEERED PROCESS FLOW

An example of a reengineered process is shown in exhibit 5-1. The process emphasizes simplification and integration with the human resource business process and systems.

5.7 MEASURING PERFORMANCE

Performance metrics focus on complexity. Exhibit 5-2 provides a checklist for measuring performance.

Exhibit 5-1 Reengineered Payroll Process

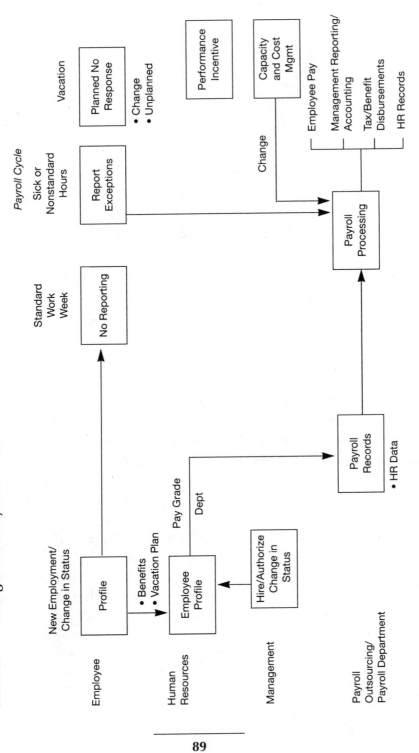

**Exhibit 5-2   Performance Measures:
Payroll**

Cost Drivers
Number of payroll cycles
Number of manually prepared checks
Number of payroll tax jurisdictions
Employee turnover
Number of benefit plans
Number of tax law changes

Productivity Metrics
Lower cost per employee
    payroll processing

Quality Metrics
Cycle time to update human resource
    and payroll systems

5.8   KEY CHALLENGES

The major challenge to payroll reengineering is the impact on the payroll department. Outsourcing will essentially eliminate the need for a payroll department. The challenge is simplifying the internal payroll process to minimize the need for manual intervention from the data source and the outsourcing vendor. Customization and maintaining vestiges of decentralized payroll departments will minimize cost savings.

On the other hand, there will be a need on the part of finance to address data and system-architecture issues for payroll. As discussed above, cost management requires a payroll process supporting activity-based management. A financial information environment that integrates process and activities with employees' department and labor costs will enhance finances' ability to improve financial and business performance through transaction data that provides business insight.

CHAPTER 6

Travel and Expense Reporting

6.1 INTRODUCTION

Travel and expense reporting and reimbursement process touches all sales personnel and all other employees who travel. The time spent finding receipts and filling out expense reports always seems excessive, and the process tedious and frustrating.

The financial impact of changes to tax regulations and stories of spending abuse have led most companies to retain tight control over expense reporting. In addition, efforts to concentrate travel-related spending to negotiate improved rates with airlines, hotels, and rental-car agencies have reinforced management's demand for intensive oversight. While the need to control travel spending is important, the issues that also need to be considered are:

- Who should be responsible for controlling travel costs—the corporation or the individual?
- What is the objective—managing travel costs or managing the total cost of doing business?

6.2 BENCHMARKING

(a) AVERAGE

The total cost of the travel and expense process is approximately .01 percent of revenues and less than 3 percent of total finance cost. For a $100 million company, this reflects a cost of approximately $10,000. For a $1 billion company, the potential cost is $100,000.

(b) WORLD CLASS

World-class travel and expense processes will basically eliminate the entire cost of the travel and expense finance process—savings approaching the cost noted above. If the priority of financial reengineering is based on total cost saving, travel and expense reporting would be assigned a low priority.

However, the major cost of travel expense reporting and reimbursement is incurred by the employees. Easily, the cost of a travel and expense report could exceed $50 per report due to the time incurred:

- Completing the report
- Obtaining management approval
- Responding to questions by the travel and expense clerks
- Receiving and depositing the reimbursement

6.3 REENGINEERING

Travel and expense reporting is the most control-laden and policy-driven financial process. Combine this control with an acute corporate fear that travel cost is difficult to control and you have a process that is the antithesis of the "control-free environment" that is required for managing a financial utility and virtual corporation.

Yet, who can argue with the need to address the problems with complying with tax laws and managing travel cost? Employee empowerment is a major component in the reengineering of financial processes; however, empowerment does not excuse employees from adhering to corporate policies and procedures. If these policies and procedures are *not related to legal, regulatory or ethical concerns*, should employee empowerment supersede these policies?

The reason for raising this issue in travel and expense reporting is the trend for corporate-mandated travel programs and policies to reduce and control travel-related expenses. Travel expenses are significant and have been managed with minimal controls by many companies. The solution has been to dictate travel policies and arrangements, shifting control responsibility to corporate. While it is clear that travel expenditures are high, we need to recognize that this is only one component of the cost of doing business.

Cost of doing business is the right number to manage. Management must have the flexibility to manage the total cost of doing business to improve competitive position and meet customer expectations. Value will ultimately determine profitability and revenue growth.

Travel and expense reporting has traditionally been the responsibility of the accounts payable department. The procedures for authorization of travel and expense reimbursement reflect a similar level of control and accounting focus; consequently, the accounts payable design objectives and best practices are applicable to travel and expense reporting.

Travel and expense process reengineering design objectives include:

- Paperless processing
- Self-authorization, that is, purchasing cards
- Outcome-based controls relying upon budgeted/forecasted spending

Leveraging technology is an important aspect of the process design because travel and expense reporting is a manual-intensive process driven in large part by tax regulations that cannot be avoided.

6.4 BEST PRACTICES

The cost of doing business is the responsibility of management. Travel and expense reengineering must be developed reflecting management and employee accountability for travel and expenses. The best practices described below emphasize employee accountability and process simplification:

- Eliminate accounts payable review and management approval of every time and expense report
  - approval based on self-authorization
  - review limited to statistical auditing
- Eliminate T&E accruals
- Download credit card information into T&E report
- Prepare on-line/remote time and expense input and validation
- Automate feed to payroll for reimbursement through accounts payable
- Minimize number of expense categories

6.5 IMPLEMENTATION

We appear to be faced with a reengineering paradox: empowering employees while requiring strict compliance to rigid policy guidelines. The solution to this paradox is found in our paradigm shift from a "process based" to an "outcome based" control environment. An outcome-based control environment expects that employees are well informed of tax regulations and will make a good-faith effort to comply with all regulatory requirements. An outcome-based control environment expects employees to be accountable for managing travel costs and corporate travel departments to offer services to help employees manage expenses.

There are only a few steps in travel and expense reporting:

1. Collecting receipts
2. Completing a report document
3. Submitting documents for approval
4. Receiving expense reimbursement

Policy and technology are integrally linked to accomplishing a successful reengineering of the travel and expense process. Following is a look at the reengineering changes by activity step.

(a) STEPS 1 AND 2

Credit card programs linked to new travel and expense software packages are allowing direct downloading of purchases to an employee's expense report—automating receipt retention and report preparation.

The new software programs are user-friendly and will classify spending by expense categories with learning capabilities. After assigning an expense category to a new travel expense, all future spending will be automatically posted to the same expense category.

Off-the-shelf software packages for personal computers now offer these capabilities, eliminating cost as a barrier to the new software technology.

(b) STEP 3

Policy changes combined with technology can eliminate this entire step, including all travel expense clerical activities. The new system would allow:

- Self-authorization of employee travel expenses
- Remote transmission of report information, automatically recording the relevant information to the accounts payable system
- Process-control focus, using statistical samplings of employee expense reports to test compliance with policy and integrity of information

(c) STEP 4

To simplify reimbursement, expenses can be posted from the accounts payable system to the payroll system, resulting in travel expense reimbursement being consolidated with payroll disbursement. Direct deposits can separate payroll and expense reimbursements to allow employees to keep funds from being intermingled.

Taking this process one step further, companies can design a process eliminating the need for employee reimbursement. Companies would take responsibility for corporate credit card payments, allowing cash advances from credit cards to cover out-of-pocket travel expenses.

6.5   Implementation

This approach requires that credit card expenditures are only for travel expenses, and the total amount of cash advances and spending must be reconciled to expense reports.

(d)   TECHNOLOGY

The technology performance requirements have been discussed above. The major issue will be driven by the technology base and strategy of your company. The technology discussed above requires either:

- Personal computers with modems to transmit data to the accounts payable system; or
- A computer network with the travel and expense software and capabilities of transmitting the data to the accounts payable system.

The cost of the technology to support a world-class travel and expense process will be driven by the availability of the above technology.

(i)   Personal Computers

The cost will be acquisition and support for the incremental number of PC's required to provide employees' access. This is not a one-to-one relationship of PC to employee. The number will be based on the employees' working environment.

For salespeople, we would normally assume a one-to-one relationship. For employees who spend the majority of their time at a company site, the number will be determined by department or site management. An operating location may need access to only one personal computer.

Assuming an acquisition cost of $2,500 per computer, a company requiring one hundred more computers to provide employee access would spend $250,000. Based on estimated annual technology support cost of $500 per computer, expenses would increase by $50,000, for a total first-year cost of $300,000—not a small number. This does not include the cost of the software, which will range from $40 to $60 per copy.

From a purely financial evaluation perspective:

1. We will assume a one-to-one PC-to-employee relationship.
2. We will estimate that each of these employees prepares on average forty-eight time reports a year. The total number of time reports is then forty-eight hundred.
3. Taking our estimated employee cost of $50 per report, the savings will be $240,000 per year.
4. By the end of the second year, company savings will be $130,000 ($480,000 minus $350,000), without including the savings associated with eliminating travel and expense processing.
5. The savings should be evaluated over a three-year period to reflect the useful life of the computer. Therefore, our evaluation will be based on three-year savings of $720,000 less computer acquisition and support costs of $400,000—a savings of $320,000 before adjusting for net present value.

(ii) Network

This is only an option if distributed systems are or will be made available. This will be solely based on your company's technology strategy. The only cost is for a site licensee for the software.

6.6 REENGINEERED PROCESS FLOW

As discussed above, the travel and expense process steps are few. The major attributes of the process design in exhibit 6-1 are:

Exhibit 6-1 Reengineered Process Flow

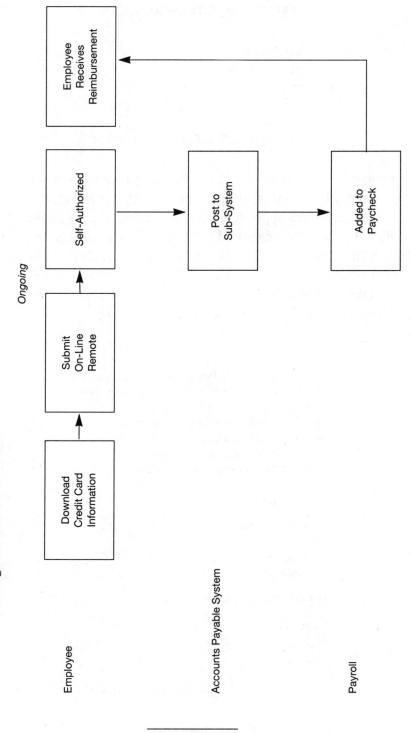

- Easy report preparation
- Self-authorization of expenses
- Paperless process

6.7   MEASURING PERFORMANCE

The measures described in exhibit 6-2 are valuable for assessing to-day's environment and creating the momentum for change.

These measures apply equally to the future. It is to be hoped that many of the cost metrics would go to zero. The net change in the each performance metric can be used to assess the quality of the reengineered solution. Even if several of these cost metrics were to go to zero, it will be important to monitor them to evaluate process integrity and remind people of these process cost drivers. (See exhibit 6-3.)

Exhibit 6-2   Key Performance Indicators

Cost Drivers
Number of reports submitted/process
Percent reports audited
Number of authorizations required
Documentation required exceeding
    IRS requirement
Number of expense categories

Productivity Measures
On-time reporting of expenses
Cost per expense report processed
Number of returned reports for correction

Quality Measures
Cycle time—process
Cycle time—pay
Percent reports submitted on time
Percent returns
Percent corrections

Exhibit 6-3   Reengineered Process

• Automated on-line input (paperless)	• Elimination of approvals
• Statistical audits	• Eliminate advances and pre-paid airfare
• Employee responsible for all T&E	• Reimbursement through payroll
• Integration with sub-systems	• Remote record retention

6.8   KEY CHALLENGES

The major challenges to successful implementation are:

1. Finance's culture, which could lead to strong resistance against:
   • self-authorization, and
   • seamless technology environment eliminating financial review of expense reports.
2. Technology environment will be a given that will require that you work within the parameters of your company's technology infrastructure and future strategy. However, you will be in a position to be a catalyst for change by:
   • cost-justifying technology improvements, and
   • encouraging management to use this to piggyback other technology upgrades that were not cost-justifiable on their own.
3. Integration of payroll and the accounts payable system and the travel and expense software with the payable systems could create a quagmire if you are not careful. The proposed systems changes cross different parts of the systems and financial organizations. Without their support, systems implementation will be significantly slowed, if not prevented.
4. If systems integration is prevented and finance continues to require processing each report, then the emphasis of the project must shift to the benefits to the preparer. Application im-

provements will make report preparation easier, which will be greatly appreciated.

These changes will also build a strong foundation for finance. A strong foundation combined with a positive attitude toward finance will create an environment that will support the transformation of financial management and decision-support processes.

CHAPTER 7

Financial Revenue Process: Accounts Receivable, Billing, and Credit Collections

7.1 INTRODUCTION

Transaction processes are inextricably linked to the business process they support. Accordingly, the quality and efficiency of these processes are, in part, driven by the overall business. This is accentuated in the sales and revenue process.

In the disbursement processes, finance has traditionally had significant influence over process effectiveness because it has been in a position to control spending. On the other hand, finance's role is significantly diminished in the sales and revenue process because it is not helping to generate revenues. In fact, many sales organizations would argue that finance is an obstacle to sales growth.

With sales and marketing driving the process and finance relegating itself to a defensive position, the financial revenue process is clearly a reflection of the sales and revenue process. It has been my experience that most sales and marketing organizations are reactive and in a state of "controlled chaos." As a consequence, the financial revenue process has been one of the least effective financial management processes.

To appreciate the challenges that finance faces in this unpredictable and constantly changing environment, the following will briefly review examples of behavior and actions exhibited by the key process members of the sales and revenue process:

- The sales organization
- The customer

(a)   SALES ORGANIZATION

The primary mission of a sales organization is to aggressively pursue its sales targets. Management is constantly developing new incentive programs and plans to motivate and direct the sales effort that range from targeting specific customers or products to just driving revenue growth. Competitive or economic pressures might lead to price changes. Confronted with the risk of losing a sale, a salesperson may negotiate special pricing or other terms—sometimes neglecting to adequately document these conditions prior to billing the customer.

The following actions initiated by the company can impact customer billing activities:

- Incentive plans often distort sales patterns, resulting in sales peaking at the end of a specific time-period identified in the plan—typically at the end of the month or quarter.
- Pricing changes can be on short notice and cover all products. If there are multiple billing systems and the applications are old, pricing changes may be difficult to implement prior to the date they go into effect.

- Customers often become irate and will short-pay a bill if the invoice does not reflect the terms and conditions committed to by the salesperson.

(b) CUSTOMERS

Customers are equally unpredictable. They may withhold payments or send partial payments for a variety of issues, including:

- Bankruptcy
- Dissatisfaction with products or services
- Product back orders
- Product returns due to warranty problems
- Disagreement over pricing or terms
- Their own internal processing errors

All of the above customer actions and how the sales organization responds can impact the credit and collections process. The possible results include:

- Changing billing terms
- Writing down receivables
- Placing a hold on product shipments or service contracts
- Sending the accounts receivable to a third-party collection agency
- Completely writing off accounts receivable—bad debt

(c) FINANCIAL REVENUE PROCESS

The ability of finance to adapt to these changing conditions can best be measured by the activity level in the accounts receivable or cash application process. The majority of the daily activity in the accounts receivable function is follow-up on cash receipts that cannot be applied against the invoices outstanding—since cash receipt matches will automatically be applied by computer systems. These errors are due to process problems in the sales and revenue process.

In short, accounts receivable process is an error-correction process—a non-value-added activity. The activity level and cost of the accounts receivable process is directly attributable to the sales and revenue process. Therefore, to reduce accounts receivable cost, the sales and revenue process must be reengineered.

Besides accounts receivable being an effective measure of the sales and revenue process, it reinforces the need to look at the finance functions supporting the sales and revenue process as an integrated process—"the financial revenue process."

7.2 BENCHMARKING

(a) AVERAGE

The total cost of the financial revenue process represents .3 percent to .4 percent of revenues and 20 percent of total finance cost. This translates into $300,000 to $400,000 for a $100 million company and $3 million to $4 million for a $1 billion company.

Other approaches to measuring cost can be on a customer or transaction basis. While the number of customers and transactions can be dramatically different from company to company with the same revenues, the average cost for processing an invoice will range from $7 to $12 for the bill and $.50 to $2.00 for accounts receivable.

(b) WORLD CLASS

Reengineering the financial revenue process as an integrated process and using the best practices described below could allow savings of

$200,000 to $300,000 for a $100 million company. For a $1 billion company, the savings could be even greater—potentially $2.5 million to $3.5 million.

The best-in-class benchmark for total finance cost is .5 percent of sales. Considering that the financial revenue process is generally 20 percent of finance's total cost, the cost target would not exceed .1 percent cost of sales of finance—which is consistent with the percentage cost savings noted above.

Long-term finance's 60 percent–40 percent cost mix favoring transaction processing will shift to a 40 percent–60 percent mix favoring the financial activities that support management efforts to improve profitability and competitiveness. Therefore, businesses should be setting a long-term cost target of .01 percent for the financial revenue process—leading to cost targets of $100,000 for a $100 million company and $1 million for a $1 billion company.

These cost targets emphasize the need for breakthrough thinking and new paradigms for the financial revenue process.

7.3   REENGINEERING

The first business issue that must be addressed is finance's role and responsibilities in the sales and revenue process. When considering finance's responsibilities, the traditional focus has been on two measures:

1. Collecting what is due
2. Minimizing the risk of bad debt

This historical definition and viewpoint of finance's fiduciary responsibilities have relegated the role to no more than that of a cashier and gatekeeper.

Notwithstanding the importance of these responsibilities, consider the premise discussed at the beginning of this book that finance's ultimate fiduciary responsibility is to maximize shareholder wealth.

From this viewpoint, finance's goals in the sales and revenue process are the same as those of all the key members of the sales and revenue process:

- Maximizing sales and profitability in the current period
- Creating a foundation for long-term growth

With a more proactive role in the sales and revenue process, finance can more easily address a number of other pressing issues facing most companies today, including:

- Understanding and managing customer and product-line profitability
- Accessing customer and product sales and related business information companywide, including international locations and divisions
- Reducing customers' cost of doing business with the company
- Integrating product and services sales and support into customers' business processes

Throughout this discussion of reengineering, the underlying assumption will be that finance's role is in sync with the goals and efforts of the sales and revenue process. Accordingly, the financial revenue process will shift from being defensive and reactive to being prospective and proactive.

The goal of the financial revenue process is to maximize:

- Business growth
- Long-term business and shareholder prosperity

Financial revenue process reengineering begins with improving the effectiveness of the sales and revenue process. The design criteria to support the sales and revenue process include:

- Customer satisfaction
- Sales and profitability growth
- The overall effectiveness of the sales and revenue process
- Managing financial risk against the business opportunity, considering:
  - risk-adjusted profitability of new business acquisition
  - risk-adjusted present value of future profits from strategic sales initiative
- Providing innovative financing and credit-risk analysis that improves the company's competitive position

Finally, the financial revenue process reengineering needs to address:

- The growing demand for financial and business information and decision support tools
- Supply-chain integration that is leading toward the virtual corporation, incorporating:
  - paperless processing
  - business process and systems integration

7.4   BEST PRACTICES

Because this section emphasizes the sales and revenue process and an integrated approach to the financial revenue process, the following is a review of best practices by the major steps in the sales and revenue process:

- Acquiring new customers and developing customer relations to create new sales opportunities
- Selling and providing products and services including the terms and conditions of verbal or written contract

- Receiving compensation and meeting customer service needs after receipt of products and services

(a) ACQUIRING NEW CUSTOMERS

Traditionally, finance's role in the customer acquisition effort has been credit review and authorization. As discussed above, the credit process traditionally focused on minimizing the financial risk of doing business with a customer—measured by bad debt and aging of accounts receivable.

This focus results in customers being the primary driver of credit management cost. For example, the cost of a credit review or collection call is not materially different for a large or small customer. The primary factor that differentiates the cost of credit management from one customer to another is the level of credit risk and payment problems.

Applying the 80/20 Rule to the financial revenue process, consider the following:

- Eighty percent of a company's revenues and profitability are derived from twenty percent of the customers.
- Conversely, eighty percent of the cost of credit management, as well as the cost of the financial revenue process, are supporting twenty percent of the revenues—and, if you're well managed, not at a loss.

The following practices and strategies will shift credit management resources to the 20 percent of customers that represent 80 percent of revenues—and an even higher proportion of profitability.

1. Establishing a two-tier customer base.
   - Tier-one strategic customers are the primary focus of the credit management. Allowing the sales and revenue process

team to work with finance to leverage credit management could:

- Increases sales and profitability by balancing higher risk financial transactions against the risk-adjusted incremental sales and profit improvement.
- Provides innovative financing solutions to create a competitive advantage.
- With tier-two customers, the focus should be on:
  - Consolidating customer base by eliminating unprofitable customers.
  - Requiring use of credit cards for all sales transactions.

2. Establishing on-line access to major credit agencies and automating the credit evaluation process to improve response time to sales representatives and customers.

3. Involving finance as a key member of the sales teams for tier-one customers, both current and targeted.
   - The sales and revenue process is the customers' procurement process. As discussed earlier, finance is a powerful instrument in the evaluation and recommendation of most major purchases. Finance could serve as a key player in the selling process by:
     - Improving the timing and quality of responses to finance's questions.
     - Building a relationship with the customer's finance organization—a key decision-making group that has been removed from the relationship-selling efforts of the competition.
   - Pairing the two finance organizations suggests that pairing members of the sales and revenue process with the customers' procurement process could improve the overall effectiveness of the revenue process. By finance initiating a peer approach to relationship-selling, finance also could be

serving as a catalyst to enhancing the overall effectiveness of a company's relationship-selling efforts.

- Providing finance with better insight to help the sales organization structure come up with innovative pricing and financing solutions.
- Finance has visibility to all the major purchasing activities across the company. From this perspective, finance's relationship approach with the customer's finance organization could lead to new sales opportunities.

(b) SELLING AND PROVIDING PRODUCTS AND SERVICES

To improve the effectiveness of this activity in the sales and revenue process, the major objectives of the financial revenue process include:

- Reducing sales cycle time
- Simplifying and minimizing the cost of customers' buy activity
- Improving the integrity and value of the financial and business information and systems environment

In response, best practice companies are:

1. Shifting to the sales and revenue process team, that is, the sales organization, financial accountability and responsibility for
   - Sales authorization
   - Credit risk
   - Working capital and cash flow
2. Integrating sales and revenue process information and systems to
   - Improve integrity of process information and systems environment by

- • eliminating duplication of work
- • minimizing errors
- Establish common data definitions and data architecture for all financial and business information in the sales and revenue process
- Provide capabilities to allow customers and the sales organization to
  - • transact business
  - • access information from order status and track relevant financial and business information

3. Establishing purchasing card programs, which are
   - Optional for tier-one customers
   - Required for tier-two customers in order to
     - • eliminate the majority of the financial revenue process cost by outsourcing financial revenue process to credit card companies
     - • eliminate credit risk
     - • improve cash flow and working capital
     - • reduce customers' cost of doing business with company

4. Consolidating the functions in the financial revenue process into a shared service environment,
   - Reducing operating cost and improving process effectiveness by
     - • leveraging scales of economy
     - • eliminating duplicate systems and processes
     - • expediting implementation of best practices across the business
   - Consolidating all sales and revenue process information and systems to
     - • improve access to companywide information in the near term
     - • provide a single focal point to drive integration of fi-

nancial and business systems and common data architecture
- build critical mass to justify technology investments and a world-class information technology support group

5. Working with tier-one customers to understand their financial and business requirements to
- Maximize the quality and effectiveness of customer service and sales support
- Implement EDI, EFT, and other related technology solutions desired by the customer: It is inadvisable to use EDI, because of the potential for embedding high-cost and ineffective management practices into the procurement process and, conversely, the sales and revenue process. The exceptions I noted in the accounts payable chapter were for industries with high-volume sales or purchases and low-dollar purchases, the rationale being that operational necessity will lead management to design an effective and low-cost process solution using EDI.
- Eliminate all non-value-added costs driven by the financial revenue process
- Define systems and information requirements to
  - integrate the supply chain
  - create a virtual financial and business environment

(c) RECEIVING COMPENSATION AND MEETING CUSTOMER SERVICE NEEDS AFTER RECEIPT OF PRODUCTS AND SERVICES

Since the activity level and the resource requirements for accounts receivable and collections are a direct result of the quality and integrity of the sales and revenue process, activity level and resources requirements are the first areas to be addressed in building best-in-class accounts receivable and collections functions.

The primary drivers of cost are:

- The number of cash receipts that cannot be automatically applied to invoices outstanding
- The number of problem accounts that require follow-up for payment

The average rate of first-time application of cash receipts to invoices outstanding ranges from 50 percent to 80 percent. It is likely easy to imagine following-up on 20 percent of all cash receipts for your company. If a company receives ten thousand payments per year, two thousand of those payments would require human intervention. This is approximately forty payments per week, or eight a day. Some of these will require three to four hours of clerical time, solving problems, calling customers, calling salespeople, and issuing credit and debit memos.

The average time to solve and correct a payment that does not match will be approximately fifteen minutes. An average of thirty-two payment problems per day will require one full-time clerk—to fix problems caused by others in the sales and revenue process. At an 80 percent rate, this equates to four hundred payments per day, two thousand payments per week, and approximately eighty-eight hundred payments per month (using an average of twenty-two workdays per month).

In addition to the above cost and productivity issues the objectives for this segment of the financial revenue process should focus on areas where finance can add value.

These objectives include:

- Maximizing cash flow and minimizing working capital requirement

- Providing post-sales and service information to monitor customer satisfaction and quality of products and services

Best practices in this area include:

1. Working Capital Management
   - Direct customer remittance to bank via lockbox, EFT, or purchasing cards to reduce cycle time of cash receipts.
     - Bank cash application will reduce the time it takes for money to be deposited by a minimum of one to two days.
     - Purchasing cards can reduce days outstanding by as much as thirty days.
     - Strategic positioning of lockboxes also can reduce the number of days that payments are in the mail.
   - Consolidation of accounts receivable systems to increase visibility of accounts receivable. Tracking payment history will allow you, with experience, to forecast cash flow on a daily, weekly, or monthly basis. Improved forecasting of cash requirements will help to minimize borrowing and, in turn, reduce financing cost.
2. Customer Satisfaction
   - Integrating the collection and cash applications into the quality management process. Since activities in this area are due to process problems, follow-up and problem resolution will become valuable information for improving the business processes responsible for the problem.
   - Recognizing that finance is one of the activities to touch the customer last in the sales cycle, a customer-driven approach to these functions will enhance customer satisfaction.
     - While resolving financial matters in favor of the customer will impact the profitability of the transactions

involved, the cost of customer acquisition will far exceed these costs. This should be seen as an investment in the customer relationship and improved customer service.

7.5 IMPLEMENTATION

There are three major reengineering areas that deserve further discussion.

1. Reducing transaction processing cost:
    - centralization into shared services
    - purchasing card program
2. Empowering the sales organization by establishing that it is accountable and responsible for:
    - financial integrity of sales results
    - credit-risk decisions
    - cash flow and working capital associates with the sales and revenue process
3. Creating a financial revenue process and process team focused on sales growth and long-term financial prosperity

The three major initiatives noted above are the mirror image of the reengineering initiatives discussed in chapter 4, the accounts payable section. Their implementation strategies and reengineering methodologies are the same. The implementation approaches and general issues are similar for both disbursements and revenues. Therefore, you should refer to chapter 4 for further discussion on implementing these three initiatives.

Nevertheless, there are unique aspects of the financial revenue process that are important to address:

1. The success of implementation will be highly dependent on the sales and process team's participation in the reengineering process.
2. Sales and senior management must accept the business implications of the new direction, including:
   - tiering the customer base
   - rationalizing the customer base
3. Strong project management and implementation schedule executions minimize disruptions to customers and the sales organization.
4. It will be a challenge to create a cohesive organization and common vision with employees that come from different finance functions and have vastly different skill levels and organizational biases.

While revenue responsibility has always resided with the sales organization, financial practices have often hindered sales performance. The goal of empowering the sales organization is to eliminate financial practices that have been barriers to sales growth.

Shifting financial responsibility to the sales organization now places finance in a position of service provider. With authority clearly with sales, the only activities that finance will perform will be those required by sales. This will provide a catalyst for sales to actively participate in reengineering the financial revenue process in order to improve sales force effectiveness.

While encouraging sales participation in reengineering efforts, these changes also pose a threat to the sales organization. Finance will no longer be a scapegoat for sales. Accountability for sales performance will clearly be in the hands of the sales organization. As sales management begins to understand the implications of these changes on performance evaluation, there will be a tendency by some in sales to want to fall back to the old financial controls and responsibilities.

Sales management backsliding will undermine the reengineering of the entire financial revenue process. The following are essential elements to success of this initiative:

- *Communication:* Accountability and responsibility for financial decisions and controls must be understood by the sales organization.
- *Change management:* Implications of changes must be accepted.
- *Financial risk management:* Balancing credit risk against sales growth opportunities to maximize sales growth and profitability.
- *Proactive member of the sales team:* Developing innovative financial solutions and building customer relationships to increase sales and enhance long-term customer relations.

Implementation must be done in the context of the overall strategy for transforming the finance function. While incremental changes associated with purchasing cards and empowerment can be moved forward, accepting finance as a partner requires senior management advocacy.

The organization is being asked to treat finance as an equal and trusted member of the management team. This requires a significant amount of effort and desire on the part of the sales organization and the sales and revenue process team. Asking management to invest time and support will require that managers believe that finance is capable of and committed to making the changes to the financial revenue process discussed in this chapter.

An isolated set of initiatives associated with the sales and revenue process will not have the weight of a comprehensive reengineering program. Finance must take a bold approach to reengineering the financial revenue process. This will require that the process changes and management framework be developed with the active involvement of senior management and the entire business enterprise.

Acknowledging that technology solutions are not a panacea, it is still important to emphasize the use of technology in the sales and revenue process. In most companies the sales and revenue process is fragmented and chaotic. Generally, production and service planning are not well coordinated with sales plans and expectations. Further, sales organizations react to customer needs rather than working with customers to understand and plan for their future needs.

By establishing financial systems integration as a major initiative, the reengineering of the financial revenue process will give finance an opportunity to be a catalyst for creating a world-class sales and revenue process. With the primary goal of the financial revenue process reengineering being to provide a foundation for improving the sales and revenue process performance, the problem is moving the dialogue from talk to action.

1. Financial revenue process reengineering provides the communications vehicle for facilitating a vision of world-class sales and revenue process for the year 2000.
2. Systems integration is a lead initiative that is tangible and will become a wedge to break through today's paradigms.

Systems integration eliminates all barriers to creating a real-time management information and decision environment. With the potential for creating a real-time, or virtual, business environment established, business process cycle time will be the major hurdle to overcome.

Cycle time is easy to measure, and it is easy to understand why it can create competitive advantage. It is a culturally neutral and unbiased measure of process effectiveness. What has been set in motion is a domino effect:

- *Systems integration:* The technology foundation for a world-class sales and revenue process in the year 2000

- *Business process management:*   The management hurdle to creating a real-time, or virtual, business environment
- *Cycle time:*   The reengineering target that measures and drives business process reengineering
- *Financial revenue process:*   The financial underpinning to maintain sales and revenue process control and integrity for a virtual sales and revenue process

7.6   REENGINEERED PROCESS FLOW

The reengineered process flow shown in exhibit 7-1 is a model of a virtual financial revenue process. The major process steps are:

1. Establishing a reliable customer relationship
2. Relying on the integrity of the business process participants
3. Monitoring and managing the activities within a process context and using plans and expected results as the primary controls

7.7   MEASURING PERFORMANCE

The form in exhibit 7-2 can be used to assess current and future performance. It can be used at various points throughout the reengineering process to track progress. As has been discussed above, cycle time will become one of the primary measures.

Exhibit 7-1 Reengineering the Financial Revenue Process

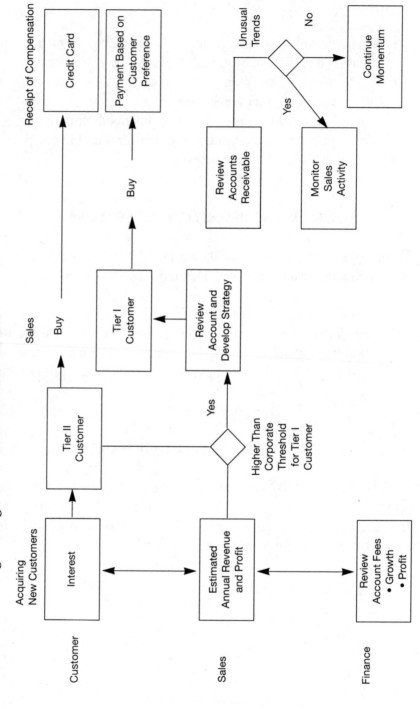

122

**Exhibit 7-2   Revenue Process
Performance Measures**

Cost Drivers
Number of accounts requiring credit review
Number of accounts with delinquent balances
Number of billing errors
Number of bills processed

Productivity
Number of accounts per customer
Dollar amounts with collection agencies
Number of accounts per credit manager
Number of accounts being managed

Quality/Service
Frequency of customer visits
Ratio of receivables to collections
• Dollar amount uncollected
• Dollar amount written off
Dollar amount accrued for bad debt

7.8   KEY CHALLENGES

As discussed earlier, some questions to keep in mind when tracking
and measuring performance include:

1. Is transformation of finance a major driver of the reengineering initiatives?
2. Has a financial systems integration plan been put in place to migrate to a single financial revenue system and processing center?
3. Have financial and business information requirements been
   identified?
4. Are financial revenue functions being consolidated?
5. Are internal controls being redesigned to empower the sales
   organization and focus on process?

Part Three

FINANCIAL AND MANAGEMENT INFORMATION

CHAPTER 8

Financial Accounting and Management Information

8.1 INTRODUCTION

When negative comments are heard regarding the finance function, they often begin with a sweeping assessment that financial managers are just accountants. Accounting stereotypes or images that are used to describe finance include:

- "Green eyeshades"
- "Bean counters"

While transaction controls and the budgeting process are the trigger for many of these comments, financial accounting provides ongoing reinforcement of this view of finance due to the accounting orientation of financial and management reporting.

Financial accounting is responsible for the integrity and reporting of financial information. As part of these responsibilities, financial accounting has traditionally provided the majority of the monthly management reporting. This limits management reporting to an accounting information structure, with limited access to operating information.

Further, the majority of accounting systems are not integrated with the major financial transaction systems, that is, accounts payable and billing; consequently, management reporting can provide only summary information of results by responsibility areas.

Information integrity is the first order of business for finance. Without the integrity of financial and management information, management cannot rely on information and financial analysis to make business decisions. Managers will then rely on their judgment and insight. If their view of the facts is consistent with reality, they will make the right decision.

Assuming you have a competent management team, consider the following comments:

- "Management does not make bad decisions based on good information."
- "Management can make good decisions based on bad information."

The latter statement is important. Judgment and insight can overcome bad information. Over time members of management will compensate for bad information by building their own information-reporting structures. Confident that their information is now good, they will continue to tolerate a weak management information environment.

The problem with this direction is that information becomes more and more convoluted. Organizations are defining their own data structures and definitions in isolation. This results in multiple management information environments that are not consistent in definition and possibly time period. This creates an even greater chasm in the business enterprise information environment—only to reinforce the dependency on the general-ledger systems for summary management reporting.

So, who's to blame for the above? Everyone. Finance for being inflexible and not advocating a dynamic management information environment. And members of management for being so frustrated that they walk away from the problem to solve their unique needs, in the process making the general management information environment more untenable.

8.2 BENCHMARKING

(a) AVERAGE

Financial accounting has traditionally been a high-cost area of finance. Financial accounting cost average is approximately .15 percent of revenues. For a $100 million company, this represents a cost of $150,000 per year. For a $1 billion company, the cost is $1.5 million per year.

This has been a high-cost area because departments:

- Have been staffed with CPAs
- Normally have a low ratio of supervision to total staffing due to efforts to retain professional staff by providing promotional opportunities
- Operate high-cost systems due to
  - high volume of journal entries because the general ledger often is the primary vehicle of management reporting
  - processing activity in turn requiring mainframe systems

(b) WORLD CLASS

World-class finance organizations are separating external and management reporting. Simplifying the chart of accounts and relying upon financial operating systems and data architecture eliminate the majority of the processing volumes and system support requirements. A world-class accounting organization is able to reduce accounting costs by as much as 60 percent or more, leading to cost savings of approximately $90,000 for a $100 million company and $900,000 for a $1 billion company.

8.3 REENGINEERING

A world-class financial and management information environment must be managed as a business process. A business process approach is important to assure that all information needs have a means of being readily communicated to those who can effectuate change.

In addition to maintaining a continuous process of communicating information requirements, the financial and management information environment can adapt to changing business requirements and grow with the business.

This process will be the enabler for using information and information technology to build competitive advantage and to maximize financial and business results, a process that will create a financial and management information environment with the following qualities:

- Timely, integrated financial and operating systems (business enterprise systems architecture)
- Reliable information
  - understood—definition of data and time period are consistent across the business

- integrity—process controls and vigilance over information environment are assured
- Accessibility
  - user-friendly query and reporting writing capabilities
  - ongoing user training and support
  - technology platform providing fast access and processing capabilities
  - executive information systems

Now, returning to the question: What is the right organization to lead the financial management information process? Financial accounting is best able to serve as process leader of the financial and management information business process.

Why is financial accounting, the "green eyeshade crowd," the right organization to lead this effort? Because the green eyeshade mentality of accountants is the most important leadership attribute for maintaining the integrity of financial and management information. This way of thinking includes:

- *Vigilance*—commitment to assuring integrity of financial and management information
- *Focus*—personal traits that allow accountants to analyze and track information at its lowest level of detail
- *Accounting*—technical skills that allow accountants to take raw data and then be able to
  - define the data
  - summarize the data into information
  - change data definitions and information to accommodate changes in rules (i.e., GAAP)
  - assure information compliance with rules
  - manage databases
  - understand the basic processes of the business from which

the financial numbers flow that make up the financial reports

The accounting department will have three major responsibilities in a financial and management information process:

1. Financial Accounting
   - preparing and reviewing journal entries to the general ledger
   - managing the monthly close process
   - maintain the integrity of the information environment
2. External Reporting
   - assuring that financial information reported to shareholders and the financial markets is in accordance with GAAP and the Securities & Exchange Commission (SEC)
   - evaluating the accounting implications of major financial and business decisions and transactions
3. Management Information
   - defining information and data elements
   - defining financial and management information requirements

Maintaining integrity of financial records requires discipline and vigilance. No other organization is dedicated to information integrity. Systems integration is allowing businesses today to develop executive information systems that overlay the integrated business enterprise system. The fast and seamless access to all financial and business information will create a greater need for management of data integrity.

Without enterprise data-integrity, management will lack confidence to rely on available financial and business information. This will defeat the purpose of a business enterprise system and, even worse, cause management to make bad business decisions.

Data integrity, business enterprise systems, and the emerging virtual business environment have created a need for an organization to take responsibility for the business enterprise information. This responsibility requires focus on detail and discipline to policies and procedures. Financial accounting is the organization best suited to take on this responsibility.

Finally, financial accounting has a strategic role in the management of the business. Financial accounting is often involved in major business decisions that will have a material impact on financial results. The bottom line impact of these accounting decisions will dwarf the dollars most financial managers and executives could ever influence. The following are examples where financial accounting's involvement would have a material impact on a company's financial results and position:

1. Mergers and acquisitions
   - asset valuation
   - good will
   - financial transaction funding source
2. Sale and disposal of business units and assets
3. SEC and GAAP accounting rule changes that have a significant impact on a company's financial position (e.g., accounting for pension liability)
4. Timing and estimation of contingent liabilities
   - regulatory investigative proceedings
   - product liability lawsuits
   - problems known internally
     - warranty
     - environmental
5. Corporate restructuring

The major goals of the financial and management information process include:

Financial Accounting
- Maintaining the integrity of financial and management information
- Same-day reporting
- No surprises
  - contingent liabilities are communicated from responsibility area when risk is first identified
  - early involvement in major decisions with accounting implications

External Reporting of Financial Results
- Reporting in accordance with GAAP and SEC
- Representing the financial position of the company to enhance market value and to provide shareholders with the insight necessary to evaluate
  - financial results and management's performance
  - the impact of management plans and actions on future value, long-term competitiveness, and general viability
- Influencing proposed American Institute of Certified Public Accountants (AICPA) and SEC rules and regulations
- Developing strong technical accounting staff

Management Information
- Assuring that financial and business information creates competitive advantage
- Real-time, on-line access to financial and operating information
- Separating accounting and management reporting
  - accounting reports focus on external reporting
  - management reports focus on business management requirements with information defined at the data element

level, eliminating information definition dependencies on the chart of accounts

8.4 BEST PRACTICES

(a) FINANCIAL ACCOUNTING: EXTERNAL REPORTING

Following are the series of best practices that will help achieve the above objectives:

- Minimize number of legal entities
- Drive chart of account requirements to expedite external reporting
- Real-time close (responsibility of financial accounting)
- Active involvement in AICPA committees
- Support extensive professional education
- Active involvement with investor relations to maximize value of financial reporting
- Provide easy internal access to financial information and related communications provided to shareholders and the financial markets

(b) MANAGEMENT INFORMATION: FINANCIAL ACCOUNTING

Best practices for financial accounting include:

- Timely processing of transactions
- Minimizing manual entries to general ledger
- Integration of subsystems to provide "drill down" capability
- Simplified chart of accounts
- Ease of maintenance

- On-line transaction edits at point of entry
- Remote access and availability
- Having subledgers send journal entries to general ledgers on a daily basis
- Providing drill-down from the general ledger to subledgers for easy analysis
- Formal training/on-line documentation
- Security and control accommodating business process reengineering and empowerment
- Data/system administration
- Elimination of overhead allocations for external reporting
- Shift of focus/data integrity to source subsystems
- Adequate security
- Reduction of cycle time to one day
- Real-time, on-line updates
- Point of entry validation
- Flattened account hierarchy (reporting structure)
- Transparent drill-downs with integrated systems
- On-line tools and PC interface with general ledger
- Reduction of accruals
- Elimination of field entries, allocations, and errors
- Better training

While the objectives may be different, the best practices for management information and external reporting are common:

- Use of noncost key performance indicators (KPIs) focused on controllable cost drivers
- Elimination of detailed variance reporting
- Use of "stoplight" reporting
- Integrated financial and operating system
- Common financial systems

- Product/customer/geographic/project/activity costs and profitability information
- Executive information systems (EIS) to support easy access to information and provide early warning
- On-line catalog of standard reports with data elements
- Historical information on-line for trends
- Drill-down capability
- Consistent definitions of financial and operational data
- Easy access for downloading and modeling
- Elimination of need for "unofficial" sources of information

8.5   IMPLEMENTATION

The best practices discussed in the previous section require a major investment of time and money to implement:

- Business enterprise systems integration
- Common data definition or data architecture
- Executive information systems with real-time and ad hoc inquiry capabilities

Referring back to chapter 2, financial and management information is the second major building block for creating a world-class finance organization. The first is transaction processing, covered in chapters 4–6.

The vision that has been laid out for financial transaction processing was developed to a great extent to achieve the above objectives. The financial utility strategy emphasizes real-time access and a disciplined financial and management information data architecture. Real-time access is dependent on a disciplined data architecture. Without discipline, information will have to be interpreted and classified as to its basic content. This intervention, such as financial classification via a chart of accounts, requires that data be held until classification is completed.

The interdependencies of transaction processing and business processing reengineering extend to financial and management information. Financial and management information is the communications vehicle for all financial and business processes. The management information strategies discussed in the earlier chapters are based on the financial and management information goals stated above.

The financial and management information process primary responsibilities are:

- *Leadership:* advocating, creating, and managing a financial and management information environment that builds competitive advantage
- *Vigilance:* maintaining the integrity of the information environment and assuring that the process adapts to change

Returning to the electrical utility analogy in chapter 4, you might consider the leadership and vigilance role as being equivalent to a public utility commission. However, in our financial paradigm, this is a shareholder wealth commission. The major objective of this commission is to assure that the financial and management information and technology environment is an enabler for management to improve operating and financial performance.

The following reengineering initiatives provide a simple road map for creating a world-class financial and management information environment that will be the distribution or communications network for the financial utility and, in turn, the virtual corporation.

8.5 Implementation

(a) FINANCIAL AND MANAGEMENT INFORMATION PROCESS IMPROVEMENTS

Many of the benefits expected from this management information environment can be demonstrated prior to making a major financial commitment. The key to implementation is to focus on the best practice process improvements that require little investment in information technology:

- One-day close—the process improvements to accomplish a one-day close are the process improvements required for a real-time close; what is missing are integrated systems to create the real-time environment.
- Simplified chart of accounts—simplify chart of accounts as first step in demonstrating the power of establishing a common data architecture.
- Define business information requirements.

(i) One-Day Close

The requirements for a one-day close are very simple; however, implementing the changes requires changing practices that are ingrained into the way people think about financial information. These steps include:

- Eliminating monthly accruals, or, at a minimum, creating statistical-based accruals
  - payables—impacting cost, inventory, and liabilities
  - receivables—impacting asset classification to cash
  - billing—impacting revenues and the cost of goods sold, which is also associated with inventory value

- Eliminating month-end manual journal entries
  - no month-end adjustments for budget reporting purposes
  - technical accruals for taxes
- Minimizing legal entities
- Implementing an automated direct recording of transaction systems to a general ledger
  - integrated and common systems are not required for one-day close
  - summary totals reported by phone or PC on first day automatically booked to general ledger without review
- Recognizing contingent liabilities when they can be estimated and determined to meet criteria for accrual—the end of the month is no longer the trigger for estimation and determination of need to accrue for liability
- Simplifying and consolidating chart of accounts across all reporting locations
- Providing all reporting locations with on-line access to general ledger that has remote journal entries

(ii)   Simplified Chart of Accounts

The biggest challenge to simplifying the chart of accounts is educating management and staff that the data architecture will be the means for consolidating information for management reporting.

- Begin with emphasis that chart of accounts is for external reporting purposes and that in the future data definitions will provide basis for management reporting.
- Limit chart of accounts to two digits, reinforcing external reporting purpose.
- Highlight chart of accounts complexity created by management request and actions:

- new information requirements
- restructuring or acquisitions
- comparison of total number of distinct chart of accounts numbers across all reporting locations and targeted number of fifty-plus
- the higher the number of journal entries to general ledger, the more dependent management reporting is on chart of accounts and general ledger.

(iii)   Defining Business Information Requirements

With people not open to defining information to manage the business, the next step is to manage expectations while delivering short-term results.

- Begin effort as a second phase of developing the new chart of accounts
- Focus on defining information needs from transactions systems within today's accounting environment
  - simplify and build relational data elements that can be used in existing systems
  - work with primary users and customers of transaction systems to determine their business information requirements and how these needs can be supported by the information in the transactions systems

The changes to each of the financial processes discussed in this book have information and technology ramifications. However, the majority of process efficiency, or cost reduction, recommendations do not require technology but rely upon:

- Eliminating activities
- Reducing transaction volumes
- Outsourcing

The majority of the technology reengineering recommendations emphasize improved information and decision support. Because most reengineering recommendations are not dependent on investment in new technology, the benefits from transforming finance can be realized before addressing major financial investments.

During each major reengineering initiative, there must be an evaluation of information requirements and the expected benefits from improving the management information. Further, leveraging information technology can improve financial results even to a greater extent than the efficiency recommendations. But the leverage allowing this information and technology to deliver results is intangible:

- Analysis leading to insight
- Judgment
  - relying upon the integrity of the information environment
  - evaluating the analysis and insight
  - taking action
- Monitoring results and repeating cycle
- Insight gained to make better decisions

By using each reengineering initiative to support the need for a world-class financial and management information environment, a company will make the value of this information environment understood and strongly supported by all customers of finance.

The following financial reengineering solutions highlight the need for a world-class financial and management information environment.

- *Budgeting*—emphasizing performance management
  - eliminating detailed financial reporting
  - shifting management review to key performance indicators

---

systems environment that is seamless across all operational, technical, and business applications.

The purpose of this environment is to eliminate the cycle time to communicate information across all activities and processes of the business enterprise—in short, a real-time management information environment that this book has been referring to as the virtual corporation.

So the question concerning hardware is its ability to support this operating environment and the software technology applications below. Before undertaking a systems integration effort, you must have a complete understanding of your current and future business requirements. The following are only examples of some of the factors to be considered:

Telecommunications
- Customer and vendor integration needs
- Definition of timely—now, tomorrow, next month—noting "timely" may vary by activity or business process
- International requirements
- Network requirements
- Remote-access needs—telecommuters, field personnel (sales, service, distribution, etc.)

Central or Distributive Processing Environments
- Processing volume of transaction applications
- Information access needs of users
- Access and security considerations
- Network requirements
  - terminals and personal computer requirements
  - computer-support requirements in the field
  - customer and vendor integration

Software and Database Performance Requirements
- Processing speed performance capabilities
- Multitasking

- Peak-access requirements addressing number of users and response time
- Relational data environment allowing fluid access across all business applications
- Object-oriented data allowing dynamic creation of new information and unlimited views of data relationships

Systems Cost Considerations

- Administration and systems support
- User support
- Application maintenance and development
- Technology life cycle cost and business support implications

(ii) Software

Object-oriented technology is emerging as a viable technology for financial and business applications. The value of this technology is its ability to adapt to the user's environment without major investments in systems design and development. There is still significant time required for installing the applications, but this time is put to good use if focused on understanding your business requirements and the specific activities and associated information requirements.

This sounds similar to the relational databases and systems applications in the market today. The major difference is that object-oriented technology is not constrained by software design constraints embedded in the business applications. The fact that objects or events can be defined translates into an application that can be modified by the events or information needs of the business without rewriting or customizing systems applications. In other words, the emergence of object-oriented financial applications is to provide businesses with financial applications that can be installed today and modified, at will, to fit the needs of the activities and functions using the software.

The easiest way to describe object-oriented technology is that it is a learning system. As new activities or information events are identified, the system can be easily modified in a real-time setting to define this new event and related data and how it is linked with the information hierarchy of the enterprise. If the information can be linked to this hierarchy, the system will automatically remember the information data definitions. The data architecture hierarchy maintains an integrated information environment, thus allowing immediate access to new information and data definitions as they are created.

This information is accessible even if you do not know it exists. While relational database applications allow for self-learning, the ease and speed of object-oriented software technology is unparalleled. This is because object-oriented technology eliminates constraints inherent in any application design where the basic applications logics are embedded in the software, thus requiring systems support to modify the application for existing or new business requirements that may span one or more business processes and associated software applications.

(iii) Data Architecture

All of the above technology can be leveraged only to the availability of comparable data.

The major problems facing most finance organizations has been that the chart of accounts rather than the base elements of data has been used as the classification methodology across business systems. For instance, customer codes often vary if there are multiple billing systems. Vendor codes will vary between payable systems and purchasing systems. Inventory coding for operations will vary from the inventory coding used in the cost-accounting systems. Consequently, any attempt to compare data from two or more systems becomes so difficult that it is not done.

The major problem with relational database technologies today is the expectations being built around the availability of information that has not been available before. This will be the case if you design a single, integrated system where all operation and business systems are included and data definitions changed to be common across all systems. If common definitions are not established, many will develop translation tables that will relate vendor and customer codes for analysis purposes. While this will work, it is another processing step. It also will mean ongoing maintenance of two different data sources, which over time will result in a deterioration in the quality of the translation.

Without creating a common information environment, how will you really know what your information technology requirements are? Further, by eliminating much of the transaction volume from financial reengineering and establishing a common data definition or data architecture environment, you may find that the scale and process capabilities of your technology environment may be much less than expected—helping to reduce your technology investment.

In addition, the focus of your information technology requirements definition will be better tailored to business requirements. The building of a business enterprise data architecture requires defining business and financial information requirements, which is in turn based on the business process and financial performance requirements. Consequently, after completing a data architecture initiative, you will understand how information will be used to manage the business, and, in turn, the performance characteristics of the technology platform to support this information environment will be defined.

Finally, if you create a business enterprise data architecture environment, many of the anticipated benefits can be realized. The issue then changes to defining the specific performance requirements associated with the use of the information, making technology requirements definition and selection fast and simple.

The organization will already know what data it needs and what the data sources are—operating systems and business processes. Data will be accessible, even if the process of getting it is slow. This will allow people to focus on performance needs rather than on the allure and their imagination of what technology will do to solve their needs.

Understanding how data is used to manage business results will shift the selection process to evaluating technology based on the performance characteristics of the software and hardware technologies and how they interact with each other and the user community.

Technology decisions should not be made in an environment where business processes are weak and information requirements are not clear. When technology is selected to solve today's problems, the technology solutions end up focused on yesterday's problems, not today's or tomorrow's business and financial requirements. Consequently, you are not only investing time and resources on yesterday's problems, but you also are undermining the willingness of senior management to make future investments in technology when the results expected do not materialize.

Even if the technology does meet the results expected, management expectations will not be met, because today's problems are different from the problems you fixed.

In short, financial reengineering combined with creating a business enterprise data architecture must be under way and delivering results before you address the business enterprise information technology environment.

If you wait—until you have fixed many of the problems and understand the future business and information requirements—the benefits of the information technology will be tangible and be viewed as an investment in building a stronger and more competitive business enterprise.

8.6 REENGINEERED PROCESS FLOW

The process flow in exhibit 8-1 is designed to reflect a "lights-out" information processing environment. Data integrity is the responsibility of the financial and business processes. Information and data architecture are consistently defined, allowing immediate access to consistent and comparable information. Systems information and common financial applications, when combined with the above information management environment, create a real-time, or virtual, information environment.

Exhibit 8-2 highlights the process flow for a real-time close process, which is essential to a lights-out transaction environment. The key to this process is to limit manual journal entries to material changes and to recognize one-time events immediately after the financial impact can be estimated.

8.7 MEASURING PERFORMANCE

The primary focus should be on access time to business enterprise information requested. Access time to information should be in nanoseconds. Because a real-time access environment is emphasized, a comprehensive solution will be required. Until all aspects are implemented, performance will continue to be in variance with management's expectations, thereby keeping pressure on the financial and management information process to see the implementation to its completion. (See exhibit 8-3.)

Further, as the business information needs change, the real-time information measure will flag needs for change.

Exhibit 8-1 Reengineered Process Flow—Management Information

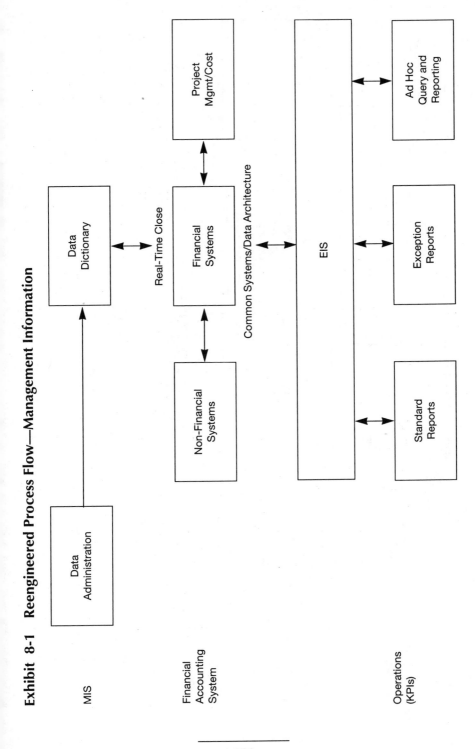

Exhibit 8-2   Reengineered Process Flow—Financial Accounting

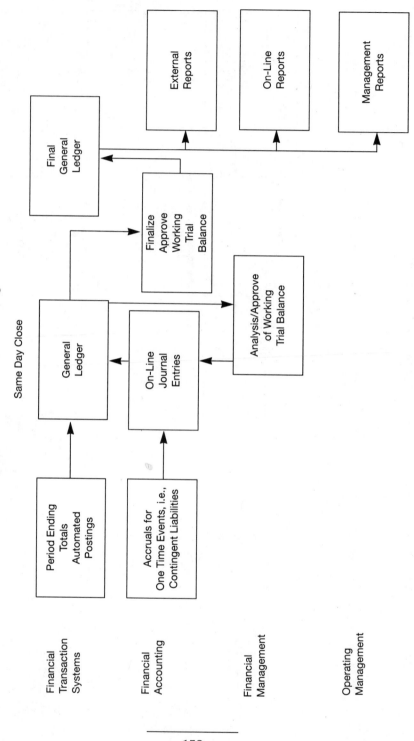

Exhibit 8-3   Key Performance Indicators: Financial Accounting and Management Information

FINANCIAL ACCOUNTING

Cost Drivers
Number of transactions (line item)
Number of journal entries
Number of people entering journal entries
Number and complexity of allocations
Number of accounts in GL
Number of new accounts
Number of accounts budgeted
Number of changes in budget and forecast
Number of non-value-added changes
Number of independent GLs

Productivity Measures
Cost/transaction
Percent transaction automated
Percent transition allocations
Cost of maintenance
Processing time

Quality Measures
Number of manual
   journal entries
Number of adjustments/errors
Closing cycle time

MANAGEMENT INFORMATION

Cost Drivers
Number of pages created
Number of budgets and forecasts
Complexity and detail of budgets and forecasts
Number of departments
Number of products and services
Level of reporting detail
Frequency of reporting
Data accountability

Exhibit 8-3 *(Continued)*

Productivity Measures
Time spent rekeying data
Percent time ad hoc reporting

Quality Measures
Timeliness/cycle time
Reporting link to KPIs
Accuracy
Business insight
Ease of use
Number of informal reporting systems
Exception reporting
• Ratio of financial/business information
• Accessibility of information for ad hoc requests

8.8   KEY CHALLENGES

The major challenge is to stabilize today's financial and management information environment by:

- Reengineering the financial transaction processes to improve process and information integrity and speed access time to information
- Implementing the following recommendations:
  - one-day close
  - simplified chart of accounts
  - defined business information requirements in conjunction with an established business enterprise data architecture

In a stable environment, finance will be better positioned with management to define current and future business requirements. With an information strategy focused on business requirements, management will be able to reduce the time to make a decision to undertake a major systems initiative and the time for implementation.

The financial and management information environment will dictate:

- The value finance will contribute to the business enterprise
- The technology and process environment necessary for a lights-out virtual finance organization

CHAPTER 9

Fixed-Asset Accounting

9.1 INTRODUCTION

Fixed-asset accounting is a very small organization in large companies and an activity of general accounting in smaller companies. The cost of the fixed-asset activity or organization is not significant; however, the responsibilities of this function can have a material impact on the financial results and position of a company.

Fixed-asset accounting is responsible for:

- Capitalization of tangible and intangible assets
- Accounting valuation (original cost, less depreciation or amortization) and depreciation expense for
  - external reporting in accordance with GAAP

- local property-tax assessments and insurance based on replacement value
- federal tax depreciation and timing difference to external reporting
- Definition of purchases and projects that require capitalization and the required documentation

The above responsibilities have a material impact on:

- *Financial results*—depreciation expense, property taxes, income taxes
- *Financial position*—long-term assets, less depreciation
- *Cost recovery*—insurance payments for property losses

9.2 BENCHMARKING

Although fixed assets are typically a low-cost financial function, representing less than 2 percent of finance cost, there are nevertheless opportunities for improving both cost and business effectiveness.

9.3 REENGINEERING

We have already discussed the significance that the fixed-asset process can have on the bottom line. The other major issue is the dollar spending threshold requiring:

- Spending approvals
- Capitalizing purchases and project spending

9.3   Reengineering

The capitalization rules can create a bureaucratic quagmire for those who are involved in the acquisition of capital assets. The low dollar limit forces management to go through a lengthy and bureaucratic process. Low dollar limits are frustrating and pose a road block that slows local or departmental business decisions and potentially limits management's ability to respond to competitive pressures.

Consider the cycle time associated with the approval process for capital projects:

- How many executives are required to sign authorization?
- How many times does finance question the project assumptions?
- How many times has maintenance spending been denied, resulting in operations waiting until the maintenance problem becomes an emergency?

Capital spending is a game between cat and mouse in many companies. While capital budgeting will be addressed in chapter 18, it is important to realize that a low limit creates excessive work that is non-value-added.

The fixed-asset process is in fact a capital management process. The quality of the management process can improve competitive advantage in both financial terms and by improving the effectiveness of the business processes needing capital funding.

The major goals for the fixed-asset process include:

- Timely and accessible fixed-asset information
- On-line, real-time environment
- High-dollar threshold for capitalization
- Process and systems integration with capital budgeting and management

In reviewing the impact of fixed-asset accounting on your business, the key issues are

- Appropriate level of control and detail over tracking of assets
- Capital management

The major cost driver in fixed-asset accounting is the amount of assets capitalized and tracked through a tagging system. Because of the need to minimize expenses and maximize control over property, companies have historically capitalized assets at very low dollar levels. However, maintaining and tracking low-value assets can be pointless, because small-dollar-value assets tend to be moveable fixtures or portable office and computer equipment. Such low-dollar assets are much more costly to track because of their sheer volume and the difficulty of locating items when auditing property inventories.

9.4   BEST PRACTICES

Best practices emphasize the need for disciplined project management, such as:

- High capitalization threshold
- Integrated capital project management system with payables and purchasing systems
- Post-audit of major projects
- Monitoring of obsolete/spare equipment
- Automatic month-end posting of depreciation
- Capital project management responsible for preparation of capitalization journal entries and supporting documentation

9.5   IMPLEMENTATION

Many companies have capitalization thresholds beginning at $1,500. The major dilemma we are facing with the capitalization threshold is profitability and financial strength, reflected by the balance sheet.

The choices are:

- *Current-period expense*—reducing both profitability and shareholder equity
- *Future-period expense*—increasing current-period profitability and shareholder equity, but also increasing fixed cost

Most companies react by deferring as much current-period expense as possible, which justifies, to their thinking, taking advantage of all spending that could qualify as a capital asset. At the same time, these companies also are trying to reduce taxes and will take an aggressive position of increasing the current-period expense for tax reporting.

Thus, the companies pursue both choices: the first choice for external reporting based on GAAP, and the second for taxes.

In either case, the impact of the cash position of the company is not affected—only which category of cash was used.

The less game-playing you do with your financial statements the better:

- Shareholders will have more confidence in the integrity of the financial position of the company—reducing their financial risk from surprises.
- Financial statements will more accurately reflect the current operating results.
- Senior management will be sending a message to the shareholders and operating management that the management team

is focused on delivering results and that poor performance will not be hidden or tolerated.

So what is the right threshold? Ask yourself whether the spending is:

- An investment in the future
- A product with a short life cycle that has become a normal cost of doing business (e.g., personal computers)

For companies with sales of more than $100 million, a capital threshold of $10,000 is recommended. This threshold should be considerably higher for companies with sales of more than $1 billion.

Although the threshold may appear high, it will instill the need for a disciplined budgeting process. Spending decisions will be better thought out because the impact on operating expenses will be immediate. Further, the threshold will help control and reduce fixed cost.

Low-dollar capital purchases can creep up on management because of the heavy emphasis on managing operating expenses. Depreciation expenses are generally excluded from departmental operating budgets. Therefore, not only will these expenses be excluded from a department's current operating expenses, they also will never be incurred in the future. This creates an attitude that fixed costs are fixed and not controllable in the near term unless there is a corporate restructuring.

The slow build on fixed cost, resulting from the above management practices, leaves little choice but to address the problem with a corporate restructuring. Unfortunately, when cost has built to this breaking point, eliminating jobs becomes part of the solution. By separating depreciation cost from operating budgets, trade-offs between investment in capital and employee costs are not adequately addressed.

For spending more than $10,000, there will be more attention paid to capital decisions. By setting a goal of eliminating 80 percent of the capital spending request, there will be fewer requests and the spending levels will be high enough to encourage a thorough review of spending proposals.

Major problems for the individual preparing the journal entries to capitalize a project are:

- Information is provided after the project is completed.
- Records of spending and use of internal resources can be incomplete.
- The individual responsible for monitoring spending is not responsible for preparing the documentation support for preparing the journal entries.

To the point, the fixed-asset staff and systems are generally not integrated with capital project spending. Single capital purchases are not a problem, but a capital project lasting for one month or more is a different story. Capital project spending can be wide-ranging: contractors, subcontractors, engineering firms, purchased material and equipment, company employees' time, and so on.

A project management system that is integrated with the fixed-asset system can provide the fixed-asset department with all the documentation necessary to capitalize the project.

Current financial and project management software allows for easy tracking of capital spending and related equipment. The software should have the ability to capture spending through the accounts payable system and track legal commitments for future spending through the purchase order system. It should monitor capital by these standards:

- Budgeted commitments and timing
  - both capital and expense
  - completion date

- Project tracking
  - spending to date
  - future contractual spending commitments
  - percent completion
  - performance of the above against budget commitments

The software should afford easy access to multiple users from engineering and from the operating location where the project is taking place. Users should not be able to create independent management information databases that cannot be reconciled with one another. Working off a common database and system will allow for better coordination and more effective management of capital spending.

The challenge in training is to assure that professional employees are up-to-date on both state and federal tax changes in capitalization, depreciation, and amortization of both tangible and intangible assets. The stronger the professional training, the more fixed-asset accounting can move from a recordkeeping and management support function.

9.6   REENGINEERED PROCESS FLOW

The major attributes of the fixed-asset process, shown in exhibit 9-1, are:

- Integration with capital management process
- Timely and accessible system with data and systems architecture designed to allow capital and fixed-cost analysis by locations and management responsibility areas (e.g., departments and business processes)
- Simplified recording

Exhibit 9-2 shows the steps involved in the reengineering process.

Exhibit 9-1   Reengineered Process Flow

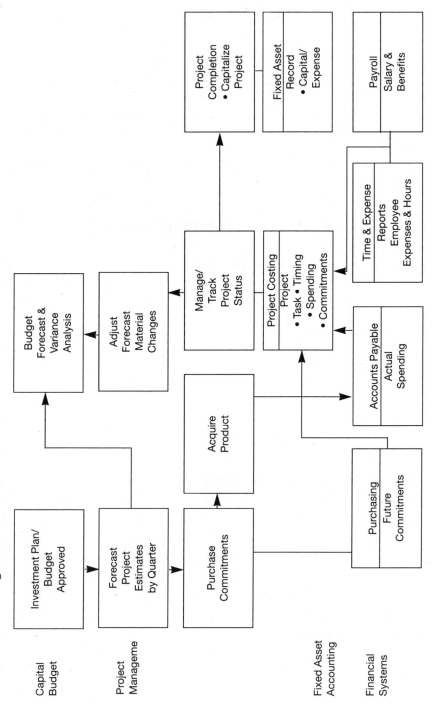

Exhibit 9-2 Reengineered Process

• No month-end cutoffs (continuous process)	• On-line request and approval per budget
• Paperless	• Access to subledger for query
• Report-writing capability	• Integrated with the general ledger
• Automated input	

9.7 MEASURING PERFORMANCE

The performance metrics in exhibit 9-3 emphasize:

- Cycle times
- Activity level
- Data integrity—measured by compliance activities and errors

9.8 KEY CHALLENGES

The major challenge to reengineering the fixed-asset process is the level of visibility you want to raise regarding the changes. Many of the process issues that we have discussed are directly related to accounting policy.

Given the visibility of capital projects in a company, along with their tax ramifications, there is more effort to comply with corporate and accounting policies. Consequently, a change in policy will impact management practices and behavior. The overall goal of this change is to reduce bureaucracy and paperwork—a goal that no one will argue with.

Further, a higher capitalization level for the management of the

Exhibit 9-3   Key Performance Indicators

PROCESS

Cost Drivers
Number of asset items
Number of projects
Number of projects approved outside
   the budget
Capitalization level policy
Percent assets depreciated vs. amortized
Number of projects included

Productivity Measures
Capital request processed
Percent time spent
Percent of request not in budget

Quality Measures
Completed projects not
   capitalized
Tax penalties
Asset disposals not recorded
Percent project cost variances from
   approved costs
Tagging/location accuracy
Cycle time
Good lease vs. buy analysis
   process

business would reinforce a more aggressive tax position attempting to minimize capital spending for tax purposes.

A year after the policy changes go into effect, management will become more aware of the impact of a higher capitalization threshold. At this point, increasing awareness of the trade-offs between expense and capital will provide the business climate to begin to challenge how capital is used in relationship to current and future overhead cost. Emphasizing the need to manage fixed cost will force management to address the fixed cost that will be built into a company's operating cost as a result of capital spending.

All of these issues should be openly discussed at the time of the policy changes. Emphasis should be on discussion, not a major theoretical argument concerning the benefits of changing capitalization policies. However, a year from the policy change, management will be in a better position to address the more strategic objectives related to building fixed cost.

CHAPTER 10

Tax Planning and Compliance

10.1 INTRODUCTION

As the title indicates, tax function has two major responsibilities:

- Planning
- Compliance

Planning: The objective of tax planning is to minimize taxes. The major activities of planning include:

- Analyzing new legislation
- Developing legislation

- Analyzing merger and acquisition opportunities
- Identifying and capitalizing on tax loopholes

Compliance: The objective of the tax compliance activity is to pay the exact amount of taxes owed. In conjunction with tax planning, the compliance process payments and tax filings will be based upon one of the following:

- Standard interpretation of tax rules and regulations
- Corporate tax position that reduces the amount of taxes owed based on the standard interpretation

The major tax compliance responsibilities include:

1. Proper treatment of state and local sales and franchise taxes for both sales and purchases
2. Property and business inventory tax assessments and appeals
3. Completing tax packages or answering questions to support the preparation of state and federal income tax returns

10.2 BENCHMARKING

The cost of the tax department is minimal, typically representing less than 5 percent of the total cost of finance. But this 5 percent of finance is responsible for managing tax liability that is a major percentage of total corporate profits. Therefore, the key benchmark must be an effective tax rate.

10.3   REENGINEERING

Minimizing taxes requires that tax and business management work together. Integrating tax planning and management is easier said than done, however.

Most finance and business managers have little understanding of tax. It is an enigma to most financial professionals. Lawyers or accountants committed to careers in tax, and corporate tax professionals, are usually isolated from middle and line management. Tax counsel has been a corporate function dedicated to servicing the upper echelons of management; however, a significant proportion of division and line management makes decisions daily that affect tax liability without benefit of tax counsel.

How can a high-profile area with a significant impact on profits distributed to shareholders be nearly invisible to most financial and business executives?

Tax typically reports to either legal counsel or to the chief financial officer. This reporting relationship alone suggests a difference in the nature of the function. Tax is a legal function focusing on the interpretation of statutes, regulations, and litigation. Committed to minimizing tax liability, the tax professional must have a thorough understanding of a business and pending business decisions to evaluate and make recommendations on tax policy and decisions.

Because the focus of tax is legal research and interpretation, compliance, and litigation, it is an island in the financial community, often spending more time with legal counsel and outside governmental agencies than with finance and operating management.

Isolation is a major difficulty in reengineering the tax function. Managing an effective tax rate and minimizing tax requires both technical excellence and active work with and support for the operating/line management. Tax issues should be addressed at the initiation of a project rather than after a decision is made. Reengineering must begin with the recognition that both tax and operating/financial management are equally accountable for tax liability and the tax implications of management decisions.

Too often, division/operating management is evaluated against operating profits before taxes. The idea is that corporate rather than operating management should be the driver of tax policy and evaluate the tax implications of major business decisions. But, every day, management decisions have an impact on tax liability:

- Location of facilities
- Lease-versus-buy decisions
- Cross-border procurement and sales agreements
- Joint ventures and strategic alliances
- Restructuring
- Capital spending
- Product development and research

These decisions are often made with tax as an afterthought. The argument is that we should not let taxes influence business decisions, but the goal of business is maximizing shareholder value and return on equity. Given that taxes are a major cost of doing business and a significant factor affecting profits available for distribution to shareholders, effective tax management must be seen as a major measure of financial management performance.

Minimizing the cost of doing business will transform tax from a technical specialty isolated from the business to a management process aimed at improving business and financial results.

This will require a seamless process that can be leveraged by operating management. The process design objectives require:

- Shifting the evaluation of tax performance from minimizing taxes to minimizing the cost of doing business

- Tax and operating management will have the same goals, encouraging cooperation.
- Tax planning will be within a business context emphasizing planning as a service for operating management, and a lever to improve operating results.
- Including tax as an operating cost requiring management to treat tax as
  - a controllable cost that should be managed like all other costs
  - a tool that can be used to build competitive advantage

10.4   BEST PRACTICES

Best practices emphasize the need for strong technical competency and communication of tax issues to division/operating management to enable proactive tax planning.

- Technical competence
  - active training and education
  - professional education credentials
- Capabilities to drive planning and tax strategy, leveraging outside expertise
- Proactive education and communication program with corporate and division finance personnel
  - tax policy
  - legislative/regulatory trends
  - personal tax trends
- Alignment of tax professions with division and corporate customer
- Tax information systems and management

- reliability and accessibility to financial transactions and results
- automated preparation and filing

10.5 IMPLEMENTATION

There are two major reengineering initiatives that require further discussion:

1. Outsourcing tax compliance
2. Treating taxes as a controllable operating cost

(a) OUTSOURCING TAX COMPLIANCE

The constant changes to local, state, and federal tax laws and regulations demand constant attention to laws and regulations and to governmental actions. This challenge has become untenable for companies with numerous operating locations. Constant changes combined with the number of operating locations increase complexity exponentially. This increases the likelihood of noncompliance and reduces the likelihood that corporate monitoring will flag noncompliance.

When factoring in that most companies' state and local tax compliance activities are not well coordinated between corporate tax and the operating locations, noncompliance is inevitable. Further, the complexity and disjointed management of the process create a high amount of non-value-added cost, including the tax fines for noncompliance.

All of the above has resulted in the outsourcing of state and local tax work becoming a major business. A company with a dedicated business aimed at state and local taxes can:

- Spread the cost of monitoring tax changes across multiple businesses
- Justify investment in technology due to critical mass
- Institute management practices taking advantage of scales of economy

The outsourcing vendors can not only reduce the cost of managing compliance, but also improve the effectiveness of tax management by improving compliance rates and taking advantage of local regulations to reduce tax cost that might not be spotted by an organization with limited resources.

(b)   TAX AS A CONTROLLABLE OPERATING COST

The technical and legal complexity of taxes has encouraged a view that managers should not be held accountable for the tax ramifications of their daily business decisions.

However, management is responsible for areas that are much more complex and technical than taxes, for example, engineering, science, and systems technology. Although management may not have these specialty skills, it will nevertheless be held accountable for the impact these professionals have on business results.

Further, a good case can be made for including tax as a controllable operating cost.

- Operating management cost responsibilities will be aligned with management responsibilities to the shareholder.
- Federal tax savings go directly to shareholder equity, compared to operating cost improvements that will be reduced by being taxed.

The goal is to maximize shareholder wealth. Because of the system of double-taxation, corporate taxes and taxes on dividends, less than 50 percent of profits will be available to the shareholders after taxes are paid.

Tax issues should not be made so complicated that they become overwhelming, but members of management need to understand the impact of taxes on the shareholder so that they will treat taxes as an operating cost deserving attention equal to its impact on operating cost and profitability.

To minimize the overwhelming potential associated with taxes, outsourcing state and local tax compliance should be the first order of business. By taking away the focus on the high-transaction activity of state and local tax at both the tax department and the operating locations, outsourcing will eliminate the majority of the noise associated with tax management. Once this is done, tax planning can be seen as a professional resource available to improve business performance.

This will require that tax planning be measured by its impact on reducing the total cost of doing business. Tax people will then have to understand the business and discuss taxes in a business context. Thus, tax will be, and will be recognized as, a service organization committed to improving business and financial results.

To support an operating cost view of taxes, taxes should not be reported "below the line." How taxes are reported will influence management's sense of responsibility for managing their cost. Above-the-line reporting of taxes will reinforce a new view of taxes as being controllable and deserving equal consideration as other operating costs.

In conjunction with this new environment, tax professionals must improve communications to the entire financial community. A proactive information program will be important to keeping people apprised and interested in tax issues—spicing this program with personal income tax tips and information will help sustain interest.

Tax professionals should be assigned responsibility for division and operating locations to encourage a client relationship. This should include charging fees for tax services to encourage tax professional interest in the business and to remind operating management that tax advice is a professional service and should be used to improve results. If management has the final choice over the level of tax support, it also will have final responsibility for tax cost. If managers choose not to use tax advice and their tax costs increase dramatically, their operating performance will be so penalized. In short, giving operating managers both choice and accountability will lead them over time, if not immediately, to seek tax advice and counsel as a normal management activity.

10.6 REENGINEERED PROCESS FLOW

The reengineered process flow emphasizes outsourcing to minimizing tax operating cost and activity. The other major process attributes emphasize communications and client-professional relationship management. (See exhibits 10-1 and 10-2.)

10.7 MEASURING PERFORMANCE

The performance metrics (see exhibit 10-3) reflect the impact of complexity on managing tax operating cost.

10.8 KEY CHALLENGES

The major challenges will be with the tax organization.

First, outsourcing will eliminate the majority of the staff and daily activity of the organization.

Exhibit 10-1   Tax Planning Reengineered Process Flow

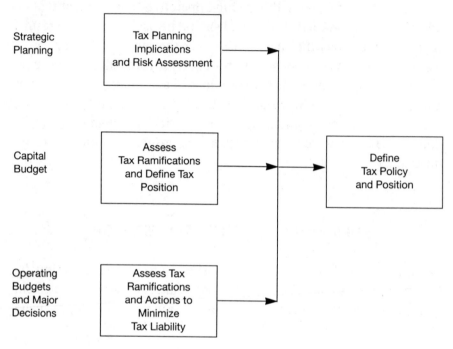

Second, shifting the emphasis of tax management to business results and client relations will be challenging for those who have been isolated from the business and have focused daily on the tax accounting.

However, many tax organizations are managed by lawyers or have several lawyers on staff. Lawyers by their training are more relationship-oriented and usually have a strong understanding of business—especially given that law school dedicates a significant amount of time to business law, commercial relationships being the primary driver of litigation.

Thus, the challenge will be to tap into the business-oriented members of the tax department. Transforming the tax process from being isolated and technical to being a more robust business process will

Exhibit 10-2   Tax Compliance—Reengineered Process Flow

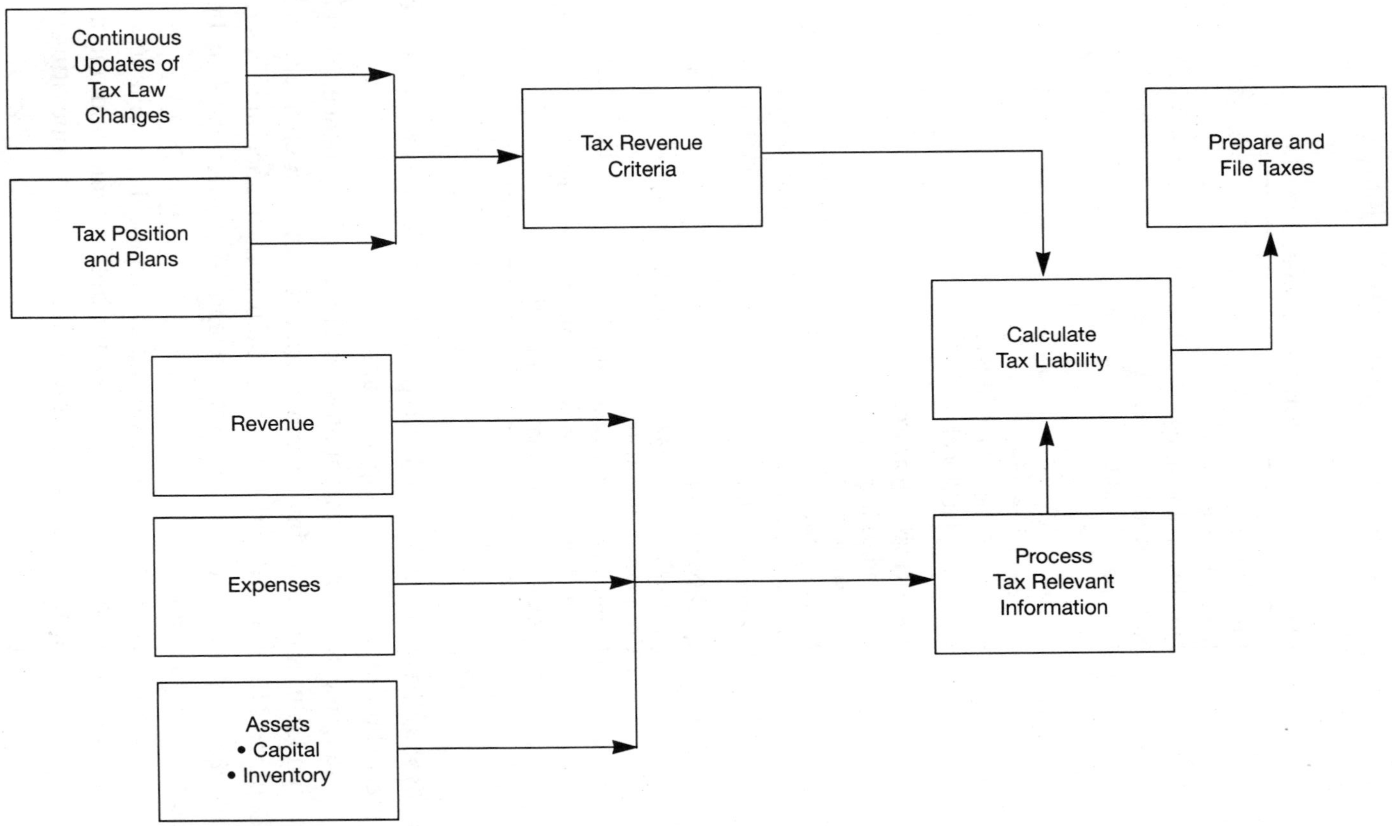

Prepare and File Taxes

Calculate Tax Liability

Process Tax Relevant Information

Tax Revenue Criteria

Continuous Updates of Tax Law Changes

Tax Position and Plans

Revenue

Expenses

Assets
• Capital
• Inventory

Exhibit 10-3   Performance Measures: Tax

Cost Drivers
Number of states
Number of countries
Number of legal entities
Number of audits
- State
- IRS

Number of people
- Federal/state income
- State/local

Productivity Measures
Audit adjustments
Extensions
Filing cycles
Automation of returns
Amended returns

Quality/Service
Accessibility of financial information to tax
Communication with divisions
Minimization of tax liability
Leveraging tax strategies to improve returns on
   business or investment initiatives

appeal to these executives and will provide management with a strong internal political base to support change.

Tax, like so many of the small specialty areas of finance, can have a significant impact on financial performance and shareholder wealth. Looking at tax at a macro level will help both finance and business management begin to realize that tax can be a lever used to build competitive advantage.

Streamlining and outsourcing state and local compliance will eliminate the drudging aspects of tax for both finance and operating management. Emphasizing the proportion of total operating cost that taxes represent will not only raise managers' awareness, but also allow them to see taxes as an untapped opportunity to reduce cost.

The bottom line is the bottom line. Emphasizing taxes as part of operating management's bottom line will allow companies to align the decisions of senior management and operating management and at the same time will raise attention to the fact that all cost and capabilities of the business must be applied to maximize results for the shareholder.

CHAPTER 11

Internal Audit

11.1   INTRODUCTION

The elimination of internal controls is dramatically changing the management control environment. Today's internal control environment emphasizes the need for documentation, authorization, and separation of duties. This results in a paper-intensive financial transaction process, in order that the auditors, internal or external, can test the validity of financial and business transactions:

- Proper authorization
- Proof of receipt or sale of goods and services
- Compliance with terms and conditions of contracts and corporate policies

- Financial recognition compliance with corporate policy and GAAP.

Spurred by financial reengineering and the requirements for creating a virtual financial transaction environment, the new management control environment will require a systematic understanding of the linkages of financial transactions with the business processes they support. This will require that all the management systems/ processes be evaluated in total to assess the effectiveness of the management control environment for each financial business process.

Statistical process control, budget to actual performance, and evaluation of the integrity of the people managing the process will become key elements of the internal control process. The challenges facing the internal audit function include:

- Redefining the financial paradigms that have dictated today's internal controls to address business process integration, corporate restructuring, outsourcing, and centralization of financial and business administration
- Committing the management talent and resources necessary to creating a business leadership role for internal audit
- Establishing a management environment emphasizing the linkage between empowerment and accountability
- Shifting the emphasis of the audit process from compliance testing to improving business process effectiveness and integrity of the management control environment

11.2 BENCHMARKING

Internal auditing typically represents less than 3 percent of total finance cost. Though the cost is not significant, many companies have been outsourcing the internal audit function. This is in great part due to internal audit functions serving as only an extension of the external audit process. Compliance testing, although necessary for the external audit, does not add value to the management of the business and is accordingly a candidate for outsourcing.

11.3   REENGINEERING

A common theme throughout this book has been the need to understand and address the interdependencies of the finance processes. The internal or management control environment supporting the twenty-first century virtual corporation will take advantage of these interdependencies by developing an integrated control model where the effectiveness of the individual controls is dependent on the effectiveness of the entire control environment. This model includes:

- "Control-free" financial transaction
- "Intervention-free" management information environment
- "Expected-outcome" control environment based on management commitments

To create a control-free financial transaction environment, the model has shifted the focal point of internal controls from the individual transaction to the integrity of the financial transaction process. The process-control approach to financial transactions allows for the creating of an intervention-free financial and management information environment. Conversely, the timely recognition of financial transactions is critical for monitoring and evaluating financial transaction activity against plans.

While the control for transactions is managing the process, the model relies upon expected outcomes of management commitments, such as forecast and budgets, to identify financial transactions that are inconsistent with the expected results—serving as a red flag for control problems. Conversely, the expected-outcome reliance on management accountability requires a barrier-free, no-excuses decision environment that empowers management to initiate the appropriate actions to meet its commitments. Further, empowered organizations require timely access to financial and management information to assess results against plan.

Many of the above concepts and interdependencies appear complex and might encourage skepticism. Therefore, the major challenge to implementing this new control environment is to assure that people understand and accept the objectives and control framework.

11.4 BEST PRACTICES

Best practices are going in two directions:

1. Outsourcing
2. Operational consulting

Outsourcing of compliance testing is in fact returning the compliance testing that had originally been done by the external auditors back to them. As long as internal audit focus is compliance testing of traditional financial processes, outsourcing or elimination of the internal audit functions are the best practice trends. The best of the world-class finance functions consider internal audit as the training ground for the future finance leaders. In this environment, the primary role of the internal audit is operational review and improvement. Besides providing management with valuable consultative services, finance builds leaders with hands-on operational experience—experience that is respected by line management and results in line management seeking a business-partnership relationship with financial management.

This consultative role will become more important as we move into the twenty-first century, and traditional compliance testing will diminish.

11.5   IMPLEMENTATION

(a)   CREATING CHANGE LEADERSHIP

Internal audit must be a leading advocate for reengineering, reinvention, and transformation. This will require change-management skills and the business stature to work with financial and operating management to develop a financial vision that addresses business requirements.

There must be a compelling business need creating a sense of urgency to change finance. The organization must understand and believe that change is inevitable and essential to survival for finance to successfully move to a virtual control environment.

This requires finance, in conjunction with line management, to define a financial leadership vision to meet the current and future business requirements. The financial leadership vision must emphasize empowerment, information access, and management accountability as the financial paradigms that underlie all the major recommendations and action plans. These paradigms should align with the business leadership vision, because the primary driver for reengineering and transforming the finance function is to support and enhance management's ability to improve business and financial performance.

The above is an abbreviated description of the first steps in the approach to transforming the finance function—discussed in chapter 2. The reason for reiterating the message is because the future management control environment will be dictated by how it is addressed at the beginning of the financial transformation process. Management control must be addressed head-on in the financial vision process (see chapter 2); otherwise, control will be addressed later during the process reengineering phase. Without a new management control paradigm, the process design teams will be forced to address anachronistic controls on a case-by-case basis.

Financial transaction controls can be directly related to the financial risk of noncontrol, beginning with the dollar value of the transactions. Concerned with financial risk, reengineering teams will tend to defer to existing control if there is no alternative. Therefore, leadership to break control paradigms should come from finance. However, the majority of people in finance will have the traditional control paradigms so imprinted into their view of the financial management environment that they will have as much, if not greater, unease with radical change to the current control process.

Consequently, it is imperative that the internal audit function step up to the challenge and take the lead in defining the management control paradigms for the twenty-first century. If internal audit is comfortable, all members of the business enterprise will have to face the reality that the new business and financial environment will be dramatically different and often may conflict with current financial practices and policies.

The management control environment defines our jobs by the constraints and boundaries it places upon us. In contrast, no constraints means that defining future jobs will be difficult, if not impossible. No constraints reinforces empowerment and the feasibility to compress decision cycle times to the point that the organization is managing in a virtual, intervention-free environment, an environment where the individual drives the business.

Thus, internal audit must become an integral partner in the strategic vision and transformation of finance. A control-free management environment will be implemented through the reengineering of each financial process. However, integrated management control environment must be understood at the time process reengineering begins to assure that the process design is consistent with the management control objectives and supports the control needs of other financial processes.

Therefore, the advocates for creating this management control environment must be the people with the functional and process responsibility for old control paradigms. If internal audit is the process champion for this new control environment, much of the skepticism and fear will be put to rest, releasing a powerful creative force into the reengineering process.

(b) CORPORATE AND FINANCIAL POLICIES

While being the champion of leading-edge thinking is critical, the internal audit function must assure that this leading-edge thinking is reflected in the policies and management of the internal control process. It is not good enough simply to state that the internal controls will be designed to meet these new control paradigms. The policies and procedures must reflect in style and in substance this new environment.

Corporate and financial policies have been the breeding ground for bureaucracy and control. To create a control-free management environment, it is necessary to create a policy-free corporate and financial authority environment. A dynamic, ever-changing financial transaction process requires that policy be able to accommodate and adapt to constant change. Continuous change requires corporate and financial policies that are easily accessible and quickly understood.

This requires a simple and clear communication process that relies on few words and a policy emphasis that is on the expected results or outcomes from the adherence to policy. Policies rely upon the competence of individuals to properly execute their jobs rather than dictating how people will do their jobs. An "expected outcome" approach to corporate and financial policies will require a policy framework with the following guidelines:

- *Why:* intent of the policy ideally stated in one sentence
- *Who:* simple statement of the policy, emphasizing roles and responsibilities
- *When and how:* reliance on properly trained employees to implement and assure policy compliance
- *What:* expected results that are associated with attributes that can be measured

This policy-free corporate and financial authority environment will be discussed following the above policy framework and guidelines.

Why. Corporate and financial policies must be few and broad-reaching so that people can easily relate their job responsibilities to these policies with no interpretation required. Policies should be developed using the Ten Commandments as a world-class example.

Who. It is everyone's responsibility to assure that corporate and financial policies are adhered to.

When. Vigilance requires that policies are adhered to at all times, with no exceptions.

How. Policies must be constantly reinforced through management behavior and communication—walking the talk.

What. The goal is an energetic and creative organization that is innovative and responsive to changing market conditions, which can be measured by the change in shareholder value. Performance measures that can be used to predict future changes in shareholder value include: sales and profitability growth, customer satisfaction, percent of sales from new products and services, and employee turnover.

11.5 Implementation

From an internal audit or management control standpoint, implementation of this policy framework requires a business and financial management environment that emphasizes accountability and eliminates excuses for poor performance. The major characteristics of the environment, which have been discussed throughout this book, include:

- *Empowerment.* Employees' ability to take immediate action without the consent of management
- *Process management.* Employees' ability to manage results through business process teams that provide the focus and control to manage and change business practices that directly influence business results
- *Performance tracking.* Management's ability to assess employee performance and business process integrity through the use of performance metrics associated with the employee and business process activities
- *Alignment.* Employee and management accountability and responsibility limited to what they can directly control and influence, assuring that people understand their job responsibilities and eliminating finger-pointing
- *Information.* Easy and timely access to financial and business information necessary to manage and assess employee, management, and business process performance.

While creating this business environment is a major goal of the financial leadership vision and financial reengineering initiatives, the internal audit function must now address compliance testing. Internal control compliance testing has traditionally focused on the review of internal control procedures and selecting a sample of financial transactions to assess the effectiveness and level of adherence/compliance with the documented procedures. While the concept of compliance testing will not change, what will be tested will significantly change.

In the policy-free management control environment that has been under discussion, the integrity of the control environment is dependent on an organization's ability to create and sustain a management environment that is focused on individual accountability. Consequently, the focus of the compliance testing will essentially assess the character and integrity of management, employees, and business processes.

However, internal audit's responsibilities do not stop with compliance testing. Internal audit must work with management to create this environment. Thus, a major responsibility of the internal audit function will be to serve in a consulting capacity to improve business and employee effectiveness. This will require change-management and organizational development skills to help management and employees accept and become the proponents of change.

11.6 REENGINEERED PROCESS FLOW

Internal audit best practices emphasize the need for increasing emphasis on and improving operating performance. In the twenty-first century corporation, operating performance will be driven by process improvement and organizational transformation. While the intent of this best practice remains the same, how internal audit executes its responsibilities will significantly change. The new internal audit function will require:

- Proactive leaders advocating the new control paradigms
- Consultants working with management and employees to improve business processes
- Change agents facilitating the cultural transformation associated with the new management control environment

Exhibit 11-1   Internal Audit's New Role and Responsibility Key Performance Indicators

---

Activity
Process analysis
Consulting
Cultural/change-management programs

Staffing
Staff experience (audit vs. nonaudit ratio)
Percentage of staff with graduate degrees
Percentage of staff with line/operating department experience

Controls
Size of corporate policy manual
Percentage of policies out of date
Percentage of audit sampling identifying misapplication of policies
Training requirements identified to assure staff knowledge will
    assure compliance with corporate policies
Training program to assure staff compliance with requirements

---

11.7   MEASURING PERFORMANCE

The performance metrics addressed in exhibit 11-1 emphasize the new management control paradigm and internal audit's new roles and responsibilities. The metrics reflect the systemic character of the new environment. The underpinning of this new control environment (transaction processing, information management, and management control) must be operating effectively or the integrity of the virtual finance environment will collapse.

11.8   KEY CHALLENGES

Internal audit must begin today to challenge the traditional financial control paradigms. This should include:

- Recognizing that cultural change is essential to successfully challenging the old financial paradigms
- Challenging people to develop a projection of what the potential business models will be for the twenty-first century
- Analyzing the implications of the twenty-first century business model on the internal and management control environment
- Advocating the business necessity of aggressively moving to the twenty-first century business model and control environment

The next major challenge will be to approach the internal and management controls as a financial/business process. This will require that representatives from every major financial and business process become members of the process team, with internal audit serving as the process owner. This team will be responsible for developing, managing, and improving the internal and management control environment.

This will require that the external auditors address to what extent they will rely upon internal compliance testing for external audit purposes. One approach would be not to rely upon the compliance work of the process team because the testing will be essentially a self-evaluation. A second approach, more consistent with the management control paradigms discussed in this chapter, would be to focus on the reliability and integrity of the internal and management control process and the business process team.

Finally, the challenge ultimately relies upon the chief financial officer. Much of the financial reengineering initiatives discussed in this book can be accomplished through the initiative of the employees and middle management. Purchasing cards, activity costing, travel and expense reporting, fixed assets, and so on can be started as a pilot project with little notice or fanfare. On the other hand, changing the fundamental paradigms associated with control and accountability will not go unnoticed, and, further, will require the full support of the senior management.

Strong leadership support for the paradigm shifts associated with the internal and management control process will bode well for successfully accomplishing the benefits expected from financial and business process reengineering.

Part Four

FINANCE AND BUSINESS PERFORMANCE

CHAPTER 12

Financial Planning and Analysis

12.1 INTRODUCTION

Financial planning is the focal point for changing finance's role from bureaucrat/controller to business partner/change agent. Financial planning's predominant role in annual budgeting, forecasting, and capital spending clearly sets the tone of the finance organization and how it is viewed. Combine this with the impact budgets have on careers and bonuses, and it is no surprise that line management may come to view finance with antagonism.

If this highly charged environment were not enough trouble, many managers question the fundamental value of financial planning—*and* financial planning analysts.

If you want to create a financial organization committed to building competitive advantage and being a catalyst for change, financial planning must be a critical component of your strategy.

The major responsibilities of financial planning and analysis are to:

- Improve financial and business performance
- Maximize shareholder wealth

While financial planning can identify the performance requirements and help to evaluate investment and operating decisions that will impact future shareholder wealth, normally it does not have responsibility for managing the business. Therefore, financial planning must influence management actions to successfully meet its responsibilities.

The four principal ways that financial planning influences management action are:

1. Business partnership
2. Business and financial performance reporting and analysis
3. Budgeting and forecasting
4. Cost and profitability management

(a)   BUSINESS PARTNERSHIP

A business partnership is a working relationship with management that results in improving business and financial performance and creating shareholder wealth:

- Best measured by the current and future growth in shareholder wealth

- Requiring a proactive financial management with strong financial and business experience and analytical capabilities

(b)   BUSINESS AND FINANCIAL PERFORMANCE REPORTING AND MANAGEMENT

Business and financial performance reporting and management provides an integrated operating framework that:

- Identifies the key levers of business and investment performance using cost and profitability management tools
- Influences management actions through budgeting and forecasting and financial analysis

(c)   BUDGETING AND FORECASTING

Budgeting and forecasting establishes a management accountability environment that focuses attention on delivering business results.

(d)   COST AND PROFITABILITY MANAGEMENT

Cost and profitability management provides the analytical tools and methodology to support:

- Action-based budgeting
- Business process management and reporting
- Business modeling and key performance measurements

It is the responsibility of the chief financial officer and senior financial leadership to bring together all the responsibilities and capabilities and apply them to build competitive advantage and shareholder wealth.

12.2 BENCHMARKING

Once you accept that financial planning is critical to the success of finance and an integral component of a world-class financial strategy, it is important to examine the function.

Financial planning represents approximately 20 percent of the total cost of finance. This is due in part to three factors:

- The highest salaried MBA recruits move through financial planning.
- The process is labor-intensive due to disjointed systems and continuous business restructuring.
- Work demands and deadlines are dynamic and uneven.

Only 25 percent of financial planning is in direct support of management decision making. As much as 75 percent of the financial planning is routine reporting and analysis. These other, time-consuming, activities include:

- Monthly forecasts, analysis, and reporting
- Budget processes that take four to six months to complete
- Monthly forecasts, which, due to a lack of accountability for forecast accuracy, are typically off by 10 percent to 20 percent

12.3 REENGINEERING

Value, and value alone, is the critical measure of financial planning performance. Value and creating shareholder wealth will not only affect financial planning, but also determine how finance views accounting and transactional operations.

A focus on value and wealth creation will lead finance to view information as a strategic asset and transactions as critical interfaces with suppliers and customers. Value must be directly linked to tangible results, and financial planning must be evaluated against its impact on business performance.

Without this level of commitment, finance will lack the determination to:

- Drive management information strategies that build competitive advantage
- Reengineer financial processes to break old paradigms

The challenge for financial executives is to take action. The decision not to act is still a decision—a decision that will weaken finance's performance and ultimately undermine the competitive position of the company. Today's business environment demands proactive management. Finance's actions must be based on critical success factors for your company.

If you believe finance's only contribution to competitive advantage is low cost, then outsource finance. If you believe finance's ultimate success is built on creating shareholder wealth, you must provide information and personnel to work closely with management to improve business and financial performance.

12.4 BEST PRACTICES

Best practices emphasize the shift to analysis and business leadership.

Essential to this change is a management information environment that:

- Eliminates labor-intensive reporting
- Creates a dynamic information environment where timely financial and business information is easily accessible

Management and professional development is critical to establishing a financial team that can be relied on for sound business and financial counsel. This will require:

- Giving personnel hands-on line management experience needed to develop a seasoned business perspective
- Encouraging diverse business, technical, and cross-functional experiences

Finally, empowerment is required so that the financial skills and capabilities can be applied to improve business and financial performance:

- Encouraging the evaluation of decisions beyond the numbers
- Creating a financial management safety net to encourage people to think and act boldly

12.5 IMPLEMENTATION

Employee empowerment, strong CFO support, and organizational development are essential to building a team of strong financial and business analysts. The effectiveness of finance acting as a value-added business partner will be driven by:

1. The quality and accessibility of financial and management information

2. The perceived value of the strategic financial management
   process
   - budgeting and forecasting
   - cost and profitability management
   - performance reporting and management

The value of these strategic financial management processes and of
the people managing these processes will depend upon:

- Eliminating unnecessary data submissions and budgeting iterations
- Limiting the focus of budget, forecast, and variance reports to
  the areas that individual managers can directly impact or influence results
- Stopping the cat-and-mouse game associated with budgeting
- Focusing performance reporting on key results and not meaningless detail

The types of changes that should be seen from the new financial planning and analysis include:

- Eliminating allocations of cost that cannot be controlled and
  traced on an activity basis—avoiding complexity and confusion that undermine budget credibility.
- Shifting emphasis from reporting to analysis—targeting reductions of at least 75 percent in the number of pages per report.
  (Ultimately, the standard report should be no more than one
  page, with all other data and reporting analysis developed on
  an ad hoc basis.)

- Treating the budgeting process as the bottom-up plan to achieve management's commitments to the shareholders.

The fundamental paradigm shift for financial planning is to use reporting as the trigger for analysis rather than its summation.

Beyond simplified management reporting processes and seasoned executives is the need for timely accessibility to information. With access to robust financial/management information, the organization will begin using detailed reporting as the primary mechanism for analysis and information.

(a) DEFINING THE BUSINESS PARTNERSHIP PARADIGM

With the above changes implemented, finance is now in a position to develop a partnership relationship with management. The key to a successful business partnership is that both parties must gain from the relationship:

- *Management:* receives assistance that improves business results
- *Finance:* meets commitments to shareholders and financial markets

This new relationship can be achieved only at the urging of line management. The challenge is to create an environment where management seeks finance's advice and counsel. The first step is to create a financial planning and analysis team that is customer-driven. Customers should be executives and employees who need analytical support, including:

- Executive management
- Line management
- Operations and departmental management
- Project teams

(b)   FINANCE'S RESPONSIBILITIES

The driving force for creating a business partnership is improved financial and business performance. Finance must continuously reinforce this message with a mission statement and a description of responsibilities.

Mission:
- High quality strategic and tactical business decisions
- Financial performance meeting shareholder expectations

Responsibilities:
- Value-added financial and operational analysis
  - Assessing company's strategic position
    - define strategic initiatives
    - identify acquisitions
  - Assuring integrity of forecast and budget goals to build shareholder and market confidence
  - Analyzing gaps between results, forecast, and budget goals and recommending actions
    - define strategic initiatives
    - acquisitions required
- Partnership role with operating organizations
  - key performance indicators
  - participating in key business decisions
  - understanding key business drivers

- model development
- financial training for operations management

Character of Relationship:
- Insightful analysis, financial expertise
- Communication of early warnings/opportunities by developing key performance indicators
- Translating insight and information into proactive actionable steps
- Alignment of KPIs with strategy
- Ongoing, two-way communications of strategic direction throughout the organization

Leadership Characteristics:
Finance's success in creating a business partnership that improves business results is dependent on the quality and character of financial leadership, including:

- Strong financial skills
- Broad business experience
- Self-confidence
- Commitment to improving results

12.6   REENGINEERED PROCESS FLOW

Exhibit 12-1 highlights the skill set that is required for financial planning and analysis. The skills and leadership will require a commitment to organizational transformation.

Exhibit 12-2 emphasizes the need for both building strong organizational capabilities and having a strong CFO commitment to em-

Exhibit 12-1 Financial Planning and Analysis Organization

| | Specific Skill and Experience Requirements | | | |
Sales	Marketing/Business Development	Service	Development	Subsidiaries
Pricing strategy	Strategic financial analysis	Program/project management and costing	Investment project analysis	All applicable skills for sales, marketing, service and development
Contract negotiations	Value-chain analysis	ABC/ABM	Program/project management and costing	
Decision support	ABC/ABM	Customer/product profitability analysis		
Modeling	Product profitability analysis			
Customer profitability analysis	Program/project management and costing			
Sales funnel management				

Skills and Experiences Applicable to All Positions

Practical business/operations experience	Financial and management accounting technical skill
Strong financial/operational analysis skill	Customer perspective and orientation
Strong financial planning and budgeting skill	Team member/leader orientation
Performance measurement (KPI) development	Process analysis, improvement, management experience

Exhibit 12-2 Business Partnership Financial Organization Development Model

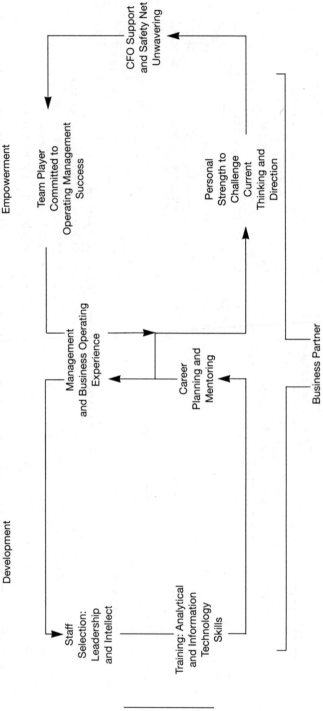

Organizational
Development

Empowerment

Staff
Selection:
Leadership
and Intellect

Training: Analytical
and Information
Technology
Skills

Management
and Business Operating
Experience

Career
Planning and
Mentoring

Team Player
Committed to
Operating Management
Success

CFO Support
and Safety Net
Unwavering

Personal
Strength to
Challenge
Current
Thinking and
Direction

Business Partner

• Improved Business Performance   • Valued Member of Management Team

Exhibit 12-3   Character of Reengineered Financial Planning and Analysis Process

• Strategic business partner with operating organizations	• More insightful analysis and strategic orientation
• Operational focus	• Proactive communication of early warnings and opportunities
• Development of key performance indicators	• Facilitate quick management decision cycle

power financial leaders. The two are critical for finance to become a valued and respected business partner.

12.7   MEASURING PERFORMANCE

The ultimate measure of financial performance is the increase in shareholder value. Exhibits 12-3 and 12-4 highlight other performance indicators that measure finance's effectiveness and transformation to business partner. The performance metrics highlight the character of the new financial planning and analysis.

12.8   KEY CHALLENGES

Business partnership is the defining moment for a world-class finance. Once finance has become a business partner, it will be in a leadership position, able to help the company meet its responsibilities to the shareholders.

Exhibit 12-4 Key Performance Indicators

Cost Drivers

Number of pages created
Number of budgets and forecasts
Complexity and detail of budgets
 and forecasts
Number of departments
Number of products and services
Level of reporting detail
Frequency of reporting
Data accountability

Productivity Measures

Time spend rekeying data
Percent time ad hoc reporting
Percent time data gathering
Percent total analysis to get needed data

Quality Measures

Good business decisions
Percent finance time working with
 operations management
Number of times asked first by
 operations management
Physical proximity to operations
Major analysis projects led/participated in
Profitability and return to shareholders
Understanding of the "whys" of the business
First to spot problems and propose actions
Diversity of business experience
Quality of personnel

12.8   Key Challenges

This relationship will lead to:

- A more competitive business
- Creation of shareholder wealth that meets shareholders' expectations
- A growth rate of shareholder value that exceeds its competition and is among the highest rate for private and public companies

A finance organization able to establish this partnership and measure its value will deliver the above results. This value must ultimately be measured by the shareholders.

CHAPTER 13

Budgeting and Forecasting

13.1 INTRODUCTION

The budgeting and forecasting process has been blamed as the embodiment of what is wrong with financial management. However, the problem is much more endemic to the overall management of the business enterprise. The budget drives management compensation; therefore, it is a major factor influencing the effectiveness of the general or business management and potentially the ability of the company to create long-term shareholder wealth.

The budgeting and forecasting process must not be taken lightly. Whatever we do to reengineer or replace this process will ultimately impact the behavior and effectiveness of management and the general/business management process.

Frustration with the budgeting process has caused many people to argue that it should be eliminated and replaced by a continuous improvement indicator, such as 5 percent sales growth. This, however, is abdication of management's responsibility to the shareholders to maximize financial and business performance. Arbitrary numbers, while they may look good in a strategic plan, are dysfunctional because they are not calibrated to the operating and competitive realities—both good and bad.

Further, much of the reengineering of the budget process has still failed to address the major flaw in the process—the lack of management accountability. Management accountability by fiat is not management accountability; it is management autocracy.

Budgeting is a high-stakes, zero-sum game, a game where decisions are taken from a standpoint of winners and losers. One organization's gain is viewed as another's loss. Commitments are made and accepted—with questioning of only those submissions that are not satisfactory. Give managers the answer they want, and they will be satisfied and ask no questions. Submissions that satisfy management are typically not questioned because those submissions become the support for satisfying the next level of management.

This "see no evil, hear no evil, speak no evil" approach creates an environment of plausible deniability. The game is tolerated until shareholders no longer will tolerate results that are below expectations. If shareholders take action and bring in a new management team or the company becomes a target, senior management takes the brunt of the failure—the same people who used this management system for years to their own advantage.

Corporate restructuring and business process reengineering have been responses to reversing the poor financial results created by this management system. In most organizations, the budgeting process has remained basically the same, with greater ability to put pressure on management to deliver results. As long as the traditional budgeting process continues in an organization, financial and business results will be suboptimized.

There have been significant improvements in corporate performance over the past five years as a result of the fundamental transformation of the business enterprise. However, companies are beginning to hit the wall. Emphasis on reducing operating costs is leading companies to restructure and spin off business or acquire competitors to take advantage of economies of scale.

Growth cannot be dictated by fiat. Good ideas, good people, good plans, and good action are all required to successfully create sustainable growth. Industry and economic growth can mask problems for a while, but eventually business performance will be dictated by the quality of management. The budgeting and forecasting process is an indicator of management effectiveness and can serve as a litmus test of those who will lead into the twenty-first century and those who will be left behind.

13.2 BENCHMARKING

The budgeting and forecasting process consumes 50 percent or more of the time of the financial planning and analysis staff. This time includes:

- One to two months dedicated to developing budgets
- Five to ten days a month
  - finalizing month-end results
  - reporting prior-period results
  - developing forecast
  - responding to management questions

World-class finance organizations are able to eliminate more than 75 percent of the time dedicated to budgeting and forecasting by implementing top-down budgeting and quarterly forecasting and minimizing budget and finance commitments to five to ten items.

13.3   REENGINEERING

The first step to building a world-class budgeting and forecasting process is the repudiation of the traditional budget paradigm. The traditional budget has lost sight of its fundamental purpose—communicating to the owners management's plans and the expected future financial performance.

No one will argue that shareholders have the right to know the plans of the business, of which the budget is an integral component. In chapter 17, Investor Relations, it is clear that those who are responsible for communicating with the financial markets and shareholders have always been acutely aware of the importance of the budget.

The chairs of the boards of directors, presidents, chief operating officers, and chief financial officers of corporations have always understood the relevance and importance of the budget to the shareholder and financial community. With growing intolerance for not meeting financial performance commitments, the budgeting process is viewed with greater trepidation. With no one between the company leadership team and the board and shareholders, combined with growing expectations that management deliver on their commitments, the budgeting process must be tackled with serious determination by all in the company.

The budgeting process, as most companies perform it today, has been flawed. The flaws, however, have been in the details and the focus. The key to successfully reengineering the budgeting process is to concentrate on what shareholders must focus on:

- Revenue growth
- Profit growth
- Strategic initiatives

The purpose of the budgeting process is to obtain management commitments that meet the expectations of the shareholders and the financial markets. By focusing on what the shareholders consider important, the budget process will take on an air of reality. Reality requires that all commitments at all levels of the organization be easily identifiable with the shareholders' expectations.

Management may not like what the shareholders expect, but managers will not dwell on or argue against those expectations. The debate moves from whether the targets are legitimate to whether the company can meet the targets set by the shareholders.

Two points are worth repeating:

1. The budget targets must be set by the shareholders and can be easily related to shareholder expectations at all levels of the organization.
2. By having the shareholders and financial markets dictate the budget objectives, the debate moves from the legitimacy of the numbers—where most organizations get stuck—to feasibility of meeting the shareholders' performance expectations.

The hardest part of any effort is getting started. When the numbers become the focal point of debate, one can never get started. The fundamental change is that the budgeting process must focus on how management will meet the budget targets rather than what the budget targets will eventually be. In an era where cycle times are a major factor in determining competitive advantage, consider the compression in the budgeting cycle time if the targets are no longer a subject of debate. The budget process immediately shifts into determining what it will take to meet the targets—an operating plan.

Since the numbers are a given from day one, there will be no misunderstanding of budget requirements from the board to field. All individuals in the organization know what they need to achieve, eliminating plausible deniability. Budgets become a formal commitment between each level of the organization to deliver the results that are needed.

A commitment-based budgeting process clearly communicates across the organization that budget commitments are no longer wishful thinking but are results for which management will be held accountable. Acknowledging accountability for results simplifies this annual process. Clear accountability for meeting management commitments allows for a focus on the business issues that must be addressed to achieve management's commitments.

If management is unable to meet the results, the goal is not to challenge the details but lead senior management or the shareholders to one of the following conclusions:

- External factors, outside the control of management, are adversely affecting commitments.
- Management is not capable of delivering the results required by shareholders.

As noted earlier, shareholders' expectations are focused on a few key measures. To clearly link management commitments to shareholders' expectations, management commitments must also be small in number. By limiting management commitments, a company can build a budget that allows field numbers to easily roll up to the performance commitments set by the shareholders.

- A small number of management commitments makes it easier to roll up budget numbers that will directly tie to shareholder requirements.
- The ability to tie these numbers also makes it feasible to develop business models and analytical tools that can measure and simulate activities and business processes, with a resulting rise in shareholder expectations and thus shareholder value.

13.3 Reengineering

The following points provide the foundation that is necessary for the strategic financial management processes:

1. A budget that must link to shareholder requirements will be viewed by the organization with serious intent and legitimacy.
2. Shareholder requirements are few and simple. With management commitments kept equally simple and focused, all levels of the organization will be able to relate their budget targets to shareholder requirements, making shareholder and financial market requirements tangible to all individuals in the organization.
3. A commitment budget is an action-based budget. Action implies results, and results imply that activities throughout the business can be monitored and measured.
4. Linkage of budget targets, across and at all levels of the organization, and simplicity, combined with the ability to measure activities and results, allows finance to model the business performance against shareholder requirements.
5. Modeling and measuring performance shifts focus of finance to determining the requirements to deliver results. Determining requirements to deliver results calls for:
    *   good financial and management information
    *   good analytical tools that can be applied to analyze this information
    *   exceptionally capable financial professionals who bring it all together with their insight and judgment to provide management with direction needed to meet shareholder requirements and to build the foundations for future shareholder wealth

The above form a viable conceptual vision for the strategic financial management processes. As the progression and dependence of these five key elements of strategic financial management have been described, it has become clear that this vision is dependent on the budgeting process. In other words, the budgeting process will make or break the strategic financial management processes.

(a) PERFORMANCE TARGETS

Establishing annual management commitments is a process intended to link all management commitments to specific shareholder requirements. This includes:

- Revenues
- Profitability
- Cash flow and financial positions
    - dividends
    - financing
    - working capital
    - capital structure
- Strategic initiatives
    - major performance goals
    - capital investments
        - infrastructure
        - products and services
        - acquisitions

The financial markets and shareholders will benchmark a company's success based on the risk-adjusted return on investment versus their alternative investment options. Assuming a free flow of capital, a poorly performing company's market value will decline in order that shareholders receive a competitive return on investment, and a top-performing company's market value will rise—as values go up, return on investment will go down, eventually reaching an equilibrium for companies with similar risk profiles.

Given the importance of setting and delivering a budget linked to the shareholders and the markets, one needs to step back and identify the key customers and their expectations, which can be seen in exhibit 13-1.

Successfully meeting customer requirements calls for a tight, inte-

Exhibit 13-1   Customers of the Budgeting Process and Their Expectations

Customers or Patrons	Expectations
Shareholders	Viable business plan
	• Meeting short-term investment requirements
	• Market valuation
	• Dividends
Bondholders	Viable business plan
	• Cash flow
	• Working capital
	• Financial structure
	• Profitability/cost structure
Board of Directors	Realistic business plan meeting
	• Shareholder requirements
	• Current operating performance
	• Strategic plans and initiatives
	• Economic, market, and competitive trends
Financial Markets	All of the above
	• Comprehensive report from management
	• Reviewing previous year's results
	• Assessing plans in light of market dynamics
	• Demonstrating a management team with integrity and open-door policy
	• Capability to deliver results

grated plan linking all business processes and functions to the commitments to the customers. The process of delivering an integrated plan must be a team effort focused on one goal: meeting customer requirements.

(b) PROCESS OBJECTIVES

Defining the objectives of the budgeting process will be critical to the successful reengineering effort. There is so much negative history or "baggage" with this process that a clear statement of the objectives will be necessary to help people to understand and believe that the process will be different.

There are two simple objectives:

1. Develop an action plan that meets shareholder expectations and builds for future growth.
2. Accurately forecast financial and business results in a reliable way that builds shareholder and financial market confidence in management and the company.

13.4   BEST PRACTICES

As has been discussed, the budgeting process is critical to creating a business management process that is focused on meeting shareholders' requirements and expectations. In order to accomplish this, financial leaders have addressed three major aspects of the budgeting process:

1. Cycle time
2. Focus
3. Performance measurements

13.4 Best Practices

(a) CYCLE TIME

There are two major benefits associated with cycle-time reduction:

1. Reducing the time and cost of preparing the budget
2. Improving the accuracy and reliability of budget commitments

Best practices related to reducing budget cycle times include:

- Top-down budgeting
  - Senior managers agree to targets at a level that they can control and speak to without backup.
  - Budget submissions are plans defining the actions and resource requirements to meet commitments.
- Budget cycle time limited to two to four weeks
  - Short cycle prevents the generation of large and detailed documents that are difficult to understand.
  - This cycle keeps discussion focused on the major issues and drivers impacting financial and business performance.
  - Commitments are limited to targets that management understands and has the ability to control and influence—aligning accountability with responsibility.
  - Senior management agrees to budget targets.
- A budget that begins six to eight weeks prior to, and is approved two to four weeks before, year's end
  - Budget assumptions better reflect the market trends and economic conditions—minimizing external business conditions as a justification of variances to budget commitments.
  - Budget commitments and assumptions are assured to be in sync with operations.

- operating cost structure
- inventory positions
- investment
- major capital projects that will impact operations
- The organization will be focused on the accuracy of its commitments since they will be measured within four weeks of the approval of the budget.

(b) FOCUS

Accountability for delivering results is the overriding concern of the budgeting process. Accountability requires that management has no easy outs to explain budget and forecast variances. Focus on a few key results and/or drivers of financial and business results eliminates excuses and encourages the budgeting process to focus on the major issues and challenges that must be addressed to achieve the budget targets and commitments that have been made by management to the shareholders.

While focus on a few key results and financial/business drivers is the most important aspect of this best practice category, it is worth noting the types of results, drivers, and commitments that are, or are becoming, the focus of management commitments:

- Financial and business results
  - Targets are controllable by the individual making the commitments.
  - Targets at the senior management level are absolute numbers rather than percentages for two major reasons:
    - to focus management attention on the relationship of resources required to readily address the total financial and business implications of budget actions, and

- to eliminate the domino effect often used to justify variance to budget. (For example, using revenue shortfalls does not relieve management of profit commitments.)
- Targets do not need backup detail for the executive to explain and evaluate commitments.
  - the major components of the target
  - the major factors that influence results
  - the major action items that will result in management achieving targets
- Targets are equal to shareholder requirements and expectations.
  - Executives are assigned leadership responsibility for each shareholder commitment.
  - Key drivers of business and financial performance are identified.
  - Drivers linked to shareholder requirements creating a business enterprise model associating management responsibilities with shareholder requirements.
  - Management budget actions identify impact on drivers that in turn are linked to shareholder requirements.

(c)   PERFORMANCE MEASUREMENTS

Over the past few years there has been increasing emphasis on using nonfinancial performance measures as part of the budgeting and management reporting processes. Balanced scorecards, key performance indicators, and cost drivers, to name a few, have been used to focus management attention on business performance. Some of these metrics have included:

- Quality, such as defects per million
- Customer satisfaction

- Market share
- Break-even

Incorporating nonfinancial performance measurements as part of the budgeting, forecasting, and management information processes is without a doubt an essential component to creating a business-driven finance organization.

The major challenge associated with performance measures is assuring that they reinforce the commitments being made to the shareholders. Chapter 15, Performance Reporting Management, will present a simple methodology for developing performance metrics linked to the budget commitments.

13.5 IMPLEMENTATION

Implementing a world-class budgeting and forecasting process requires changes to both process and culture. The two are interdependent: The process is a reflection of the culture and, in turn, the culture is a reflection of the process.

Best practices described above will be essential to reengineering the budgeting and forecasting process. To simplify the understanding and application of these best practices, a reengineering initiative and implementation should focus on the major process steps:

- Meeting with shareholders and the financial community to determine their requirements and expectations, which must be addressed through the annual operating budget
- Agreeing to meet the financial and business performance targets to meet these requirements and expectations
- Developing plans and resource requirements to meet the budget targets

- Forecasting expected results and adjustments in plans to meet budget commitments periodically during the year

Change in management principles will change perception and receptivity to change. A paradigm shift in the fundamental principles of the budgeting process will immediately change perception:

- Creating the organizational and management climate for breakthrough thinking
- Implementing a world-class budgeting process that will be essential for finance to successfully support the transformation to the twenty-first century finance and virtual corporation

There are two fundamental principles that must be adopted in order to successfully implement a world-class budgeting and forecasting process:

1. Budgets must be directly linked to the shareholders' requirements and expectations.
2. Managers must be accountable and responsible for developing the plans and resource requirements that will enable them to meet their commitments.

First, management and employees must understand that the budget and subsequent forecasts—tracking of results and modifying plans to meet commitments—are commitments made to the shareholders based on an understanding of the financial and business results expected by the shareholders. This makes it clear that the targets must be met and are not subject to argument:

- The targets are the targets—end of story.
- Anyone who does not like the targets has several choices:
  - Develop a plan that will meet or exceed the targets.
  - Develop a plan that falls short of the targets, explaining why the gap exists and leaving the board of directors with three options:
    - gap is legitimate and plans must be made to close and eliminate the gap within a midterm time frame of one to three years
    - gap is legitimate but plans cannot close the gap, requiring that drastic measures be taken—from restructuring to selling the company
    - gap is not legitimate and management must be replaced immediately
  - Resign.
- The shareholders always have the final decision, and that decision will be reflected by changes to the market value of the company.
- Budgets and forecast must be based on action plans that accurately reflect the anticipated financial and business results. These plans are simply stated, allowing:
  - plans to be monitored
  - results to be predicted

Second, management is accountable for achieving the commitments it makes. The focus of the budgeting process must be a two-way negotiation and commitment process, involving:

- The plans for achieving those results
- The resources required to support the plan

If management accepts the plans and commitments, but over the year denies the resources required to accomplish the plan, management cannot expect people to deliver on their commitments. However, if a plan is developed and the required resources are given, people will have no choice but to accept accountability and responsibility for the execution and the results of the plan.

13.6   FORECASTING PROCESS

A major assumption throughout this chapter is that the budgeting process is supported by a world-class finance organization with the analytical tools and an information technology environment. Budgeting and forecasting is the thread that pulls these skills and capabilities together so that finance can work with management to improve business results. The remaining chapters in this section will focus on how finance can build these capabilities.

With world-class capabilities, finance will have a keen understanding of business and financial drivers to advise management both analytically and intuitively. A finance organization that can quickly anticipate and respond to changing business conditions will be a finance organization that can work with management to develop budget and forecasting plans that will deliver the results.

Capabilities cannot be effectively applied or developed without a disciplined budgeting process aimed at meeting shareholders' expectations.

(a)   RELIANCE ON OPERATING PLANS

The beginning point for a successful operating budget is a reliable forecasting process. The ability to accurately forecast business performance requires that line management, not finance, is responsible for forecasting. A reliable forecast developed by line management requires that management integrate day-to-day business with financial and business monthly forecasting.

An operating plan that is tightly integrated with the monthly financial and business forecast assures that management considers the operating plans and how they drive financial and business results. This in turn allows management to treat the budgeting process as a simple extension of the monthly financial and business forecast. Although we cannot predict the future with clairvoyant accuracy, we can anticipate future performance if we have a management group that is capable of making financial and business commitments that are closely attuned to the daily operation of the business.

(b) LINKAGE TO BUDGET

There are several key elements of a successful forecasting process that are impacted by the budgeting process:

1. The accuracy of actual, versus budgeted, performance is at the top of the list of management's performance measures and compensation criteria. Demand that accuracy be the most critical performance measure of a budget and forecast. Underestimating performance expectations to "beat budget," suboptimizes financial performance by depriving resources from other areas.

2. Forecast is against management's budget commitments. A budget limited to five to seven performance targets will keep the forecast focused on the key business and financial drivers.

3. Line management is responsible for both the forecast and budget commitments. Finance's responsibility is to consolidate management's commitments into a forecast.

4. Budget use of the forecast as the initial base requires a twelve-month to eighteen-month time horizon.
5. Budget projections are quarterly. Accordingly, the forecast will be quarterly, with only changes that have a material impact on the current quarter or year's operating results triggering the development of a revised forecast.
6. Forecasts, like operating budgets, must be considered as business plans to deliver future results—not reports to evaluate the reasons for forecast variances.

(c) INTEGRATING SALES-DISTRIBUTION AND PRODUCTION PLANNING

The major problem with most financial forecasts is that they are prepared by finance. The historical view that the financial forecast is unrelated to the day-to-day management of the business is no longer acceptable. Budgeting and forecasting management performance commitments can be done only by management.

Management responsibility for forecasting its ability to meet performance targets may not seem like breakthrough thinking, but the reality is that excellent management focuses on the fundamentals. Most champion sports teams have excellent people, but the difference between good teams and the best is execution of the fundamentals. This applies equally to forecasting. The fundamental of forecasting is reliance on the sales and operation planning.

The fundamental sales and operations forecast is based on an integrated planning process where managers across all key functions work together to meet customer requirements:

*   Sales forecast based on account-planning and marketing initiatives

- Distribution's inventory ability to meet sales forecast based on existing inventories and scheduled productions
- Production schedule ability to meet distribution's inventory requirements
- Procurement requirements to meet production schedule

If any of the above cannot meet the forecast requirements, then the entire management team must adjust its plans, at the time of the forecast, to compensate for shortfalls. If, for example, distribution and production scheduling cannot meet the sales forecast for a product line, it is incumbent on the sales force to manage product demand to avoid back orders. This could be through working with key accounts to shift demand to the next month or providing incentives on other product lines to pull demand from the problem product line.

Management's commitment to the forecast is viable in this type of environment. The objectives are clear and the management team works together.

Further, this type of forecast makes financial forecasting a snap:

- Sales forecast includes product mix allowing sales and marketing to drive revenues and margins.
- Distribution forecast provides month-end inventory positions along with the cost of goods sold as relieved through inventory.
- Production forecast provides the cost basis for month-end work-in-process and raw materials inventory.

13.7 BUDGETING PROCESS

Financial management's primary mission is to increase shareholder wealth. This requires a budget that balances the costs of managing today's business to maximize profitability and shareholder value, with investments and initiatives that provide the basis for the creation of future shareholder wealth.

(a)   DRIVING SHAREHOLDER WEALTH

This balance between current-period and anticipated future-period profitability can be measured by the change in shareholder value. Combining this change with dividend is the shareholder's return on investment.

Return on shareholder investment =
(Change in market value + Dividends) ÷ Prior period market value

Therefore, the budget must be structured to manage the primary drivers of shareholder wealth.

1. Drivers of market value include:
   - current period financial and business performance
   - future expectation
   - confidence in management
2. Drivers of dividends include:
   - liquidity—working capital and short-term financing
   - financial structure—asset management and financing
   - future capital requirements
   - current financial performance
     - profitability
     - cash flow
     - cost of financing
     - access to financial markets

(b) ESTABLISHING CORPORATE PERFORMANCE TARGETS

By converting the above drivers into a business management framework and a financial model, finance will be able to plan and simulate scenarios that will lead to maximizing shareholder wealth.

With the above considerations in mind, the first step in the budgeting process is to listen. Listen to shareholders, financial institutions, and the financial markets.

Exhibit 13-2 provides a framework and financial models to begin a process of understanding the levers and performance indicators for maximizing shareholder wealth.

(i) Communication with Analyst and Rating Agencies

Throughout the year, companies meet with analysts to discuss plans and expected results for the coming quarter. These meetings have a significant impact on shareholder value. The reliability of the budget and forecast will influence the analysts.

Analysts are concerned about only a couple of things when it comes to quarterly and annual forecasting:

- Earnings per share
- Cash flow

This is a risk-averse group that will discount the integrity of forecast and business plans if management is unreliable. While short-term results and the forecast are the primary points of discussion, these meetings offer management an opportunity to listen to shareholders' concerns and expectations. Beyond the current year, analysts will be looking at product development, investment, and acquisition plans.

Exhibit 13-2 Reengineered Budgeting Process Flow

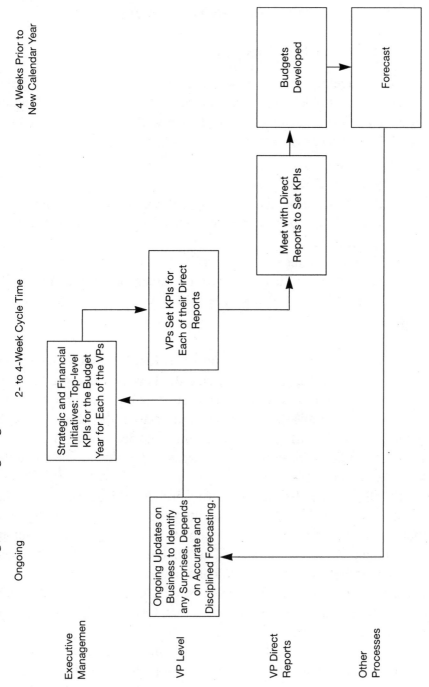

237

(ii)   Management Commitment

Senior management needs to meet annually with a select group of analysts to listen to their concerns and recommendations. After meeting with the analysts, management must meet with the executive committee of the board to discuss:

- Rating and analyst assessments
- Projected year-end results and expectations for coming year
- Strategic plan, including major initiatives and investment requirements
- Economic value of the enterprise versus market value
- Growth rate in shareholder value versus market requirements
- Potential financial and business options to maximize shareholder value

As part of this review, finance must provide the management team with the analytical insight to evaluate the key financial and business drivers. Through the use of activity-costing of business processes and the development of key performance indicators, the senior management team can identify the strengths and weaknesses that must be addressed in order to meet the expectations of the shareholders and the financial communities.

As discussed earlier, the budgeting process is dependent on the integrity and accuracy of the forecasting process. Forecasting provides management with foresight that will be the starting point for developing budget goals and targets. The analytical tools that are used throughout the year to understand and manage business and financial performance are equally important in developing the budget objectives and targets. They will be the primary analytical tools used for developing the budget action plans.

With the above completed, the senior management and the executive committee should meet to discuss current-year performance and shareholder requirements. This meeting should lead to agreement by the senior executives to take ownership for all the shareholder requirements and for the key performance drivers for which they have primary responsibility.

Executive committee involvement is based on the view that the role of the board is to maximize shareholder value rather than to serve in an oversight capacity. The board must represent the shareholders' best interests. This can be done only if the board fully understands the business.

Oversight is an important part of maintaining the viability of the stock and financial markets. However, the primary interests of the markets, in this regard, are the integrity of the financial position of the firm and the fair representation of the company's current and future viability. Assessing the integrity of the firm's financial position is the primary reason for conducting external audits.

On the other hand, fair representation of current and future viability requires that the board have a complete understanding of the business and share in the accountability for this viability. Independence only provides the board with an opportunity for plausible deniability if business fortunes reverse. Board members can blame management and the auditors for hiding facts from them. However, if the board is actively involved in setting the goals and targets of the business, along with a thorough review of the action plans, it will be fully informed as to the viability of the company.

The executive committee and the senior management team should outline the major goals and objectives for the coming year based on the above discussions. Then a company should review the recommendations with key constituencies including:

- Major shareholders
- Investment bankers
- Select group of analysts and financial advisers

Goals and objectives are finalized by the senior management team and the executive committee. Upon board approval, the budget for the year is set and the next stage is to develop plans to meet the board requirements.

The board must be aware that the goal of the process is to use the budget for developing action plans to meet shareholders' requirements, rather than arguing over the numbers. If the plans result in changes, the board must decide, as discussed earlier in the chapter, whether the management or the targets must change. However, this process is viable only if management is committed to maximizing results and the accuracy of those commitments.

(iii)   Developing Budget Plans

After management commitments have been made, each executive will prepare an action plan delineating the requirements to deliver the individual performance commitments.

Development of action plans will highlight the interdependence of line functions. Sales growth is dependent on the quality of marketing and product development. Manufacturing costs are driven by procurement of materials and resources. The traditional budgeting process tends to focus on functional cost and responsibilities. An action-based budget is implicitly a business process budget.

Business processes are the vehicle for delivering on management commitments and must also be the funding source of the activities of the process to insure a closed-loop system relative to management accountability. While action plans are an important aspect of a world-class budgeting process, without business process alignment of funding or resource authorization responsibility, a company will have a disconnect between accountability and responsibility—creating an opportunity for plausible deniability.

Staff members must see their goal as maximizing business performance rather than maintaining the departmental status quo.

In addition to action plans, the budget submission requirements should include:

- Linkage plans and commitments to the strategic plan
- Quarterly forecast of performance commitments
- Emphasis on accuracy of budget to actual

"Beating the budget" is not an acceptable world-class practice. Being under budget means that resources were withheld from other parts of the business or from the shareholders, in the form of dividends.

Throughout this process finance must meet with management to determine information requirements and identify the key performance indicators that will help manage and track the results.

A comprehensive operating plan will then be prepared and submitted to the board of directors for its review and approval. By emphasizing the key performance drivers and associated action plans, the board is in a better position to assess the viability of management commitments and, at the same time, to increase its understanding of the business.

After final approval a monthly performance report will be prepared to reflect the unique aspects of the current-year performance commitments and plans. Results will be prepared monthly with brief management commentary. Monthly reporting will focus on results not forecast. The forecast is to be done quarterly. Forecast changes during the quarter will be made only if there is a material change to the quarterly or annual forecast—up or down.

13.8 REENGINEERED PROCESS FLOW

The reengineered process flow highlights a top-down process that is focused on the key performance indicators. By focusing on performance metrics, finance can help management focus on what actions are required to influence these indicators and, in turn, meet commitments to shareholders. The top-down approach to budgeting can allow a company to complete the process in one month.

The forecasting process is conducted quarterly unless there are major forecasts to actual variances or KPIs indicate emerging trends will materially impact future results.

The reengineered process flows diagrammed in exhibits 13-2 and 13-3 are for budgeting and forecasting, respectively. A gap analysis for achieving the reengineered process is shown in exhibit 13-4.

13.9   MEASURING PERFORMANCE

The key performance indicators in exhibit 13-5 focus on (1) the level of detail and complexity, (2) the amount of rework and time, and (3) accuracy or ability to plan and forecast.

(a)   COST DRIVERS

Two major controllable drivers of cost that must be minimized or eliminated are the level of detail and starting with a bottom-up plan. Controlling these two major drivers will allow management to minimize the amount and impact of the other cost drivers.

(b)   PRODUCTIVITY MEASURES

Improving productivity requires (1) minimizing changes and (2) maximizing percentage of the controllable cost profitability to total cost profitability of the budget.

Exhibit 13-3 Reengineered Forecasting Process Flow

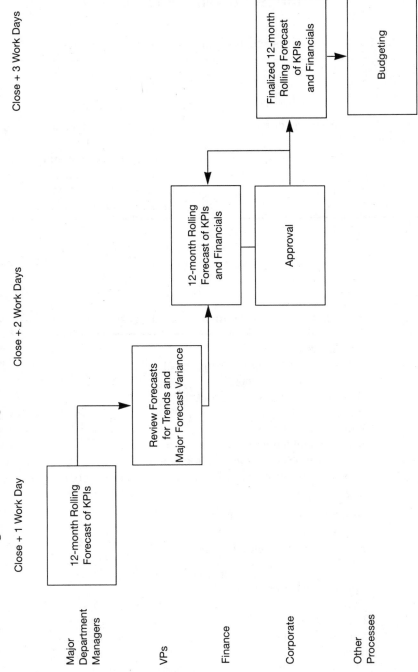

Exhibit 13-4   Reengineered Budget and Forecasting Process

Strategic business partner	Proactive analysis and communications
	More valuable analysis
Accountability based on controllable performance	Focus on operational and financial KPIs
	Focus on product-line and customer profitability
	Activity-based management basis for budget and forecast

Exhibit 13-5   Key Performance Indicators

Cost Drivers
Level of budgeting/forecasting detail
Length of formal process
Bottom-up vs. top-down process
Number of changes
Number of forecasts
Management level with budget
Number and complexity of allocations
External factors—technology, economy, competition, etc.

Productivity Measures
Number of iterations in budget cycle
Hours spent
Percent allocations/total expense
On-time submissions

Quality Measures
Cycle time
Percent differences between strategic plan and budget
Percent differences between actual budget and forecast
Validity and accuracy of assumptions
Linkage of incentives to budget and strategic plan

(c) QUALITY MEASURES

Reducing cycle time and improving accuracy of a budget/forecast are the best measures for monitoring process integrity and reliability.

13.10 KEY CHALLENGES

The biggest challenges to overcome in the budgeting and forecasting process is its historical lack of credibility and relevance to shareholder wealth. To effectively address these challenges will require a much tighter linkage of the budget to shareholder requirements. Most important, management's budgeting/forecasting must be isolated to items that it can control or influence. The higher the percentage of noncontrollable items that are included, the greater the impact on reducing the relevance and reliability of the budgeting and forecasting process.

CHAPTER 14

Cost and Profitability Management

14.1   INTRODUCTION

The typical perspective of a world-class cost-accounting or cost-management function is its ability to help management reduce cost. However, the shareholder sees cost as only a component of one of the major drivers of shareholder wealth—profitability. Profitability management is the primary objective of a cost-management activity, which is the reason for expanding the definition of cost management to cost and profitability management.

Cost and profitability management continues to evolve in parallel with the stages of business transformation.

COST AND PROFITABILITY MANAGEMENT

Stage of Business Transformation	Cost and Profitability Management
Entrepreneurial	Accounting for today's cost
Control	Cost accounting to establish budget and standard cost
Quality Management	Activity-based costing to develop product cost based on cost of resources used to support, produce, deliver, and service product
Business Process Management and Virtual Corporation	Activity-based management to develop process cost and support a business process management

Consistent with the above business stages of transformation, finance approaches to accounting for managing cost have changed over the past 60 to 70 years in parallel with the major paradigm shifts in production management. It is important to understand the relationship of cost management to production management in order to appreciate the value and capabilities that cost accounting and cost management brought to innovation and breakthrough strategies in production management.

1920s	The shift to assembly-line production required the development of standard cost.
1930s	Industrial engineering techniques provided the methodology and theoretical basis for creating cost accounting as we know it today.
1980s	Materials requirements planning, corporate restructuring, and quality management began to highlight the deficiencies of cost accounting, leading to the development of activity-based costing.
Early 1990s	Supply chain management and business process reengineering demanded process-based activity costing—often referred to as activity based.

Twenty-first century	Virtual corporation and a virtual supply chain will require a process management and process-based financial reporting, shifting activity-based management as a tool to reduce cost to the fundamental strategic financial management infrastructure to manage the business enterprise.

The above changes in the management of the business enterprise and cost and profitability management highlight a strong interdependency between management and financial theory. While management theory can lead a company to shift to new operating paradigms, finance must closely follow with a financial information system that can allow management to evaluate the financial and business results. If we cannot define a means of gathering information and data that can allow management to interpret the results of a new operating paradigm, it will be difficult to conceive of a way of managing this paradigm.

Moving forward, cost accounting will most likely not be a unique function but a major responsibility of the strategic financial management activities that are normally expected to be seen in financial planning and analysis. This chapter has been written with the view that cost and profitability management is one of the highest priorities of finance and must not be treated as a stand-alone function but as an essential tool and skill that will be a basic requirement for finance.

Best practices in cost and profitability management are:

- Activity-based management
- Project costing and management

14.2 BENCHMARKING

Cost accounting or cost management represents approximately 10 percent of finance cost and less than .2 percent of revenues in most manufacturing companies. The amount that cost accounting represents of total finance cost ranges from less than 1 percent to as high as 20 percent of finance cost.

14.3   REENGINEERING

Cost accounting has been an acceptable process for recording product cost for general accounting purposes. Accounting for cost during the early stages of the Industrial Revolution was relatively simple since product was typically created in a job-shop setting, allowing cost to be directly assigned to the product being produced.

Cost accounting, as we know it today, was developed in response to the assembly-line impact on the Industrial Revolution. Capturing cost directly associated with a product was no longer possible in assembly-line production. In order to accurately identify the cost of production, management needed a mechanism to charge indirect cost to production. Standard costs for overhead labor and materials were developed to allocate the total cost of production to product. With standardized production of components and end-products, the cost of assembly-line departments could be estimated on a per-unit basis.

In a simple one-product assembly operation, standard cost accurately reflected the cost of product. However, as we moved to more product diversification, management began to realize that costs were becoming more difficult to manage. In response to these concerns, management began to champion materials-resource planning to improve production scheduling and reduce inventory levels and operating cost. With the move to just-in-time production and the incorporation of lessons learned from numerous trips to Japan, management shifted its attentions to supply-chain management process.

While management apparently made significant improvements in manufacturing productivity and quality, the financial results did not adequately reflect these improvements. While production-line efficiency was skyrocketing, high-margin specialty products began to catch management attention. High-volume, low-profitability production was pushed aside for the high-margin specialty products that were often much more exciting due to applications of the latest technologies. Plant closings began to accelerate during the late 1980s as a result.

Activity-based costing was a new approach to capturing cost. Traditionally, fixed-cost standards were developed using labor hours as the denominator.

$$\frac{\text{Total fixed cost}}{\text{Total estimated direct labor hours}} = \text{Standard overhead rate}$$

The problem with this solution was that the major productivity improvements that were being realized from massive changes to production practices resulted in a shift in spending and labor hours to indirect cost. Higher and higher fixed cost being applied on lower and lower direct hours significantly skewed the standard overhead rate equation, especially given that better production practices resulted in fewer problems and therefore less indirect labor and management support on a relative basis to product sales.

Motivated by the high margins in more specialized products and the skyrocketing cost of high-volume production, corporate managers did not stop to think whether there was a fundamental flaw to the way they were looking at their businesses. However, once corporate restructuring took hold in the late 1980s and the expected profit improvements from plant closings did not materialize, all stakeholders in the business enterprise were ready to step back and challenge their assumptions.

The major focus of cost accounting had been on the application of standard rates against product costs using direct labor. The basic change between traditional cost accounting and activity-based accounting is the application of overhead cost.

Project teams were formed to identify the activities in the production facility and then to look at how resources were used to complete those activities, rather than allocating fixed cost simply on the number of direct hours worked. The major breakthrough was treating fixed cost as variable cost that can be applied based on the rate that resources are being used by the activities.

With activities and resources aligned, the project teams then identified the rate that products used the activities identified and thereby developed product cost based on the products' actual demands on resources. As a result of this new perspective on product cost, management in many companies began to reverse course regarding wholesale advocation of specialty products and plant closings for improving profitability.

Another major benefit of activity costing is the analytical methodologies that are used to evaluate and measure activities. Activities are classified in a variety of ways that provide insight for reengineering, cost reduction, and profitability improvements. (This classification process will be discussed in the implementation section later in this chapter.)

In the early 1990s, business process reengineering became popular. However, difficulty in managing the redesigned process led people to call for moving from a functional to a business process management structure. Further, it was at this time that frustration with activity-based costing reached the breaking point, for similar reasons. In the case of activity-based costing, the issue was that the analysis highlighted the problem cost areas from a product-cost view but did not provide a process solution to fix the problems.

Business process reengineering and activity-based costing are concerned with a common issue—managing change. Managing the changes in a future-state redesigned process environment led activity-based costing to evolve into activity-based management. With all activities of a business enterprise identified and aligned by today's business processes, finance can provide the analytical and management information tools developed from activity-based costing to manage business processes as well as product and customer profitability.

Finally, the last major cost tool that will be reviewed is for project management. As companies become more task based in the management of their businesses, business activities will come to be managed from the perspective of a project. While activity-costing methodologies support this concept, the project-costing tools allow companies to manage projects, major corporate initiatives, or programs (bigger projects) in activity-based, real-time costing and management environments. This provides a management aid as finance supports the migration of the business enterprise to process management and to the virtual corporation. The concept of process management includes continuous improvement initiatives that are aimed at changing the activities and resources used. Budgets are action plans that are to be executed by the business process management and team to improve financial and business results. In short, the budgeting process is shifting management emphasis to execution and implementation.

14.4 BEST PRACTICES

Using these tools to manage the business is what differentiates world-class companies. The essence of a world-class cost and profitability management process is that members of line management are the sponsors and advocates of activity-based management. Finance can manage the information and implementation, but the project costing tools are for managing business performance. This requires that line management uses the tools and understands the process methodology.

Consequently, the biggest problem with the implementation of activity-based management and project costing and management is limited scope of the implementation.

These tools must be a fundamental part of managing the business. World-class companies use these costing tools to manage all aspects of the business:

- Activity-based management for enterprisewide budgeting and forecasting providing:
  - product and customer profitability analysis
  - financial and management reporting to support business process management
  - data architecture definition
  - key performance indicators to support performance management
- Project costing and management for tracking and managing projects and business initiatives

14.5   IMPLEMENTATION

(a)   IMPLEMENTING ACTIVITY-BASED MANAGEMENT

There are two major challenges to successfully kick off an activity-based management initiative:

1. Line management sponsorship
2. Employee acceptance of business process analysis

The value of activity-based management is the insight that is gained from process analysis and the tools and information to take that analysis and implement change. Activity-based management constructs a tangible operating scheme for managing the business enterprise.

The *tangibility factor* is the Achilles' heel of business process reengineering. Activities and process are foreign to most employees. People tend to view their jobs in terms of their responsibilities without thinking about how to define the various aspects of how their daily activities allow them to accomplish their responsibilities. Activity-based management offers management an opportunity to transform a concept to a tangible and hands-on approach to managing the business.

The major steps for implementing activity-based management are shown in exhibit 14-1. These steps include:

- Activity definition
- Process mapping
- Process team selection
- Cost and process effectiveness analysis
- Process improvement recommendations that will be incorporated into the budgeting and forecast

(i)   Activity Definition

Implementing activity-based management requires a project approach to implementation. A core project team must be identified and assigned to the first project with the goal of taking this experience and using it to lead the next round of activity-based management implementation.

To begin, set up a departmental activity questionnaire. The objective is to identify the eight to ten major activities in the department, then to classify those activities as being value- or non-value-added. Non-value-added activities exist to correct problems. A process problem that drives additional time and effort is non-value-added. In addition to the activity definition, the activity identification phase will attempt to identify:

Exhibit 14-1   Implementing Activity-Based Management

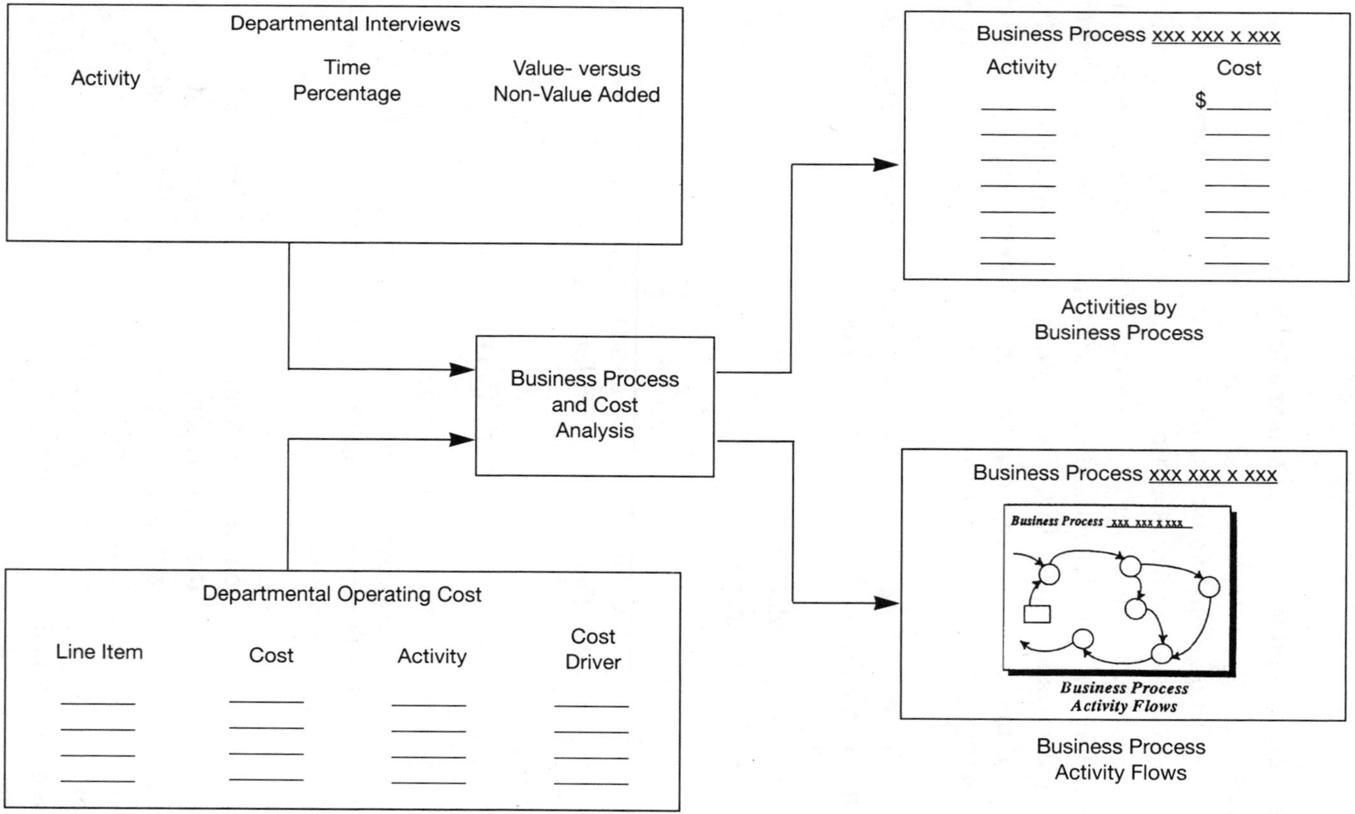

Departmental Interviews

Activity	Time Percentage	Value- versus Non-Value Added

Business Process and Cost Analysis

Departmental Operating Cost

Line Item	Cost	Activity	Cost Driver

Business Process xxx xxx x xxx

Activity	Cost

Activities by Business Process

Business Process xxx xxx x xxx

Business Process xxx xxx x xxx
Business Process Activity Flows

Business Process Activity Flows

- The number of times the activity occurs
- The inputs that trigger the activity
- The outputs that trigger the next activity
- Drivers of cost
- Performance measures to evaluate process effectiveness

(ii)   Process Mapping

With the functional interview activity questionnaires posted on a wall, the project teams will trace the inputs and outputs to the related activities. This will begin to link activities that will form a business process. The project team will now be able to analyze the process to identify and recommend potential business process leaders and business process teams.

(iii)   Process Team Identification

During the initial phase of an activity-based management project, the project teams are focused on a thorough review of the functions and line organizations in order to identify the major business processes and costs. After this first phase is completed, analyzing and making recommendations to reduce cost and improve process performance must be the responsibility of a business process team.

It is important to identify the process teams prior to conducting a thorough analysis, because they will be responsible for implementing the changes. Action-based budgets and expected-outcome control environments are all based on an activity-based management. Budgets and outcome-based controls require that process accountability start from the beginning.

(iv)   Cost and Process Effectiveness Analysis

The costs are made up of two components:

1. Direct labor cost and related benefits associated
2. Cost pools for all other costs
   - based on identifying a common variable that drives cost
   - cost driver then is used to allocate costs from the cost pools to the activities

After applying activity cost to the business processes, the business process team will be in a position to identify improvements to cost and performance based upon:

1. Activity and process cost
2. Activity attributes or characteristics
   - value- versus non-value-added
   - cost drivers—primary factors that trigger or accelerate cost
   - performance measures—assessing process effectiveness
     - cycle times
     - defects

Based upon the assessment, a business process improvement plan will be developed and will become the foundation for forecasting and budgeting.

(b) IMPLEMENTING PROJECT COSTING AND MANAGEMENT

As discussed earlier in this chapter, project costing is essentially an extension of activity-based management. Project costing and management is a structured approach to:

- Estimating and scheduling resources required to complete a project
- Monitoring and evaluating results against plan

14.5 Implementation

Project costing and management is not a new concept. However, information technology is now able to provide cost and project management tools. What has made this a best practice is information technology. Sophisticated project management software combined with integrated systems offers management a real-time information environment and management tool kit to direct daily activities and monitor progress.

Technology, however, is not the answer to effective project costing and management. Planning and accountability for execution against plan are the important attributes of a world-class project-costing and management process. Introduction of new technology offers finance the platform to raise the visibility and potential value of using project-costing and management tools.

The visibility serves as the vehicle for management "consciousness raising"—to expect better coordination and execution of projects.

The key to strong project management is planning and execution. That is all there is to it:

1. Plan
2. Execute against plan
3. Monitor results and adjust plan accordingly
4. Accountability

We are creating an environment that supports and encourages planning. Planning is a proactive approach to management that requires scheduling of resources and coordination of activities that typically cross line and staff functions. This approach is central to meeting management commitments.

In short, we are providing the management tool kit that is an enabler for management accountability. With management accountability undeniable, project costing and management will be taken seriously and efforts will be made to improve the process.

Project management is important to a wide range of business activities:

1. Product development
2. Capital spending
3. Maintenance projects
4. Special projects

Given the wide range of processes, reengineering the project-costing and management process should be a two-phased effort. Phase 1 focuses on building a foundation process and technology infrastructure that can provide basic project-costing and management capabilities. Phase 2 is customizing the project-costing and management process in conjunction with the reengineering of the specific business process.

14.6 REENGINEERED PROCESS FLOW

Exhibit 14-2 provides a process overview that treats activity-based management and project costing and management as an integrated process that is tightly linked to the budgeting and forecasting process.

In addition, this process flow highlights that activity costing combined with project costing and management is essential to creating an expected-outcome control environment. Integrity and reliability of budgeting and forecasting is dependent on the cost and profitability management process.

14.7 MEASURING PERFORMANCE

The performance metrics in exhibit 14-3 emphasize the need for simplicity and follow-through, that is, adherence to the principles and practices.

Exhibit 14-2   Cost and Profitability Management

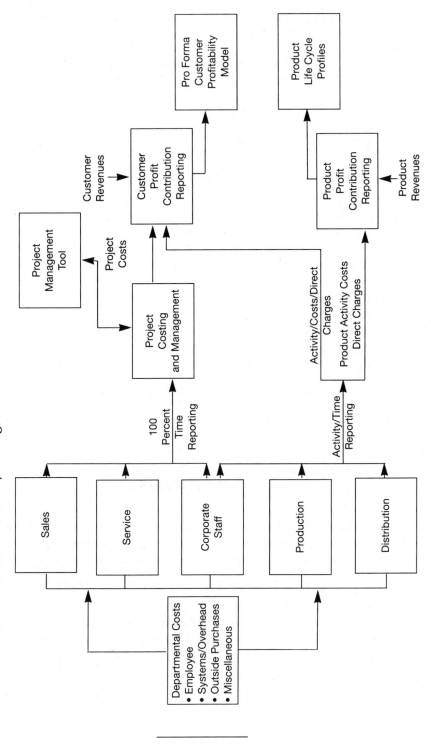

Exhibit 14-3   Key Performance Indicators

Cost Drivers
Protect costing management integration with financial systems
Level of activity detail
Number of cost allocations
Number of unique systems
Turnover of process team members
Product complexity

Productivity Measures
On-time submissions
Percent of budget/forecast using activity costing
Project forecast accuracy
Percent of projects using project costing and management tools

Quality Measures
Identification and tracking of cost drivers
Process owners
Budget/forecasting variance
Up-to-date data dictionary
Action-based budgeting

(a)   COST DRIVERS

The major driver of non-value-added cost is excessive detail. For both activities and project costing, activities should be greater than 5 percent of a department's time. The goal is to be able to understand the major influences on cost. Breaking down activities to finer and finer detail will result in an exponential increase in complexity that will require an equal increase in cost allocations and reporting. This will defuse impetus to undertake major process improvement initiatives. Complexity by its nature is a major driver of non-value-added cost for all business processes and systems.

(b)   PRODUCTIVITY MEASURES

Planning is the critical element to improving productivity of the cost and profitability management process. Therefore, the productivity measures focus on timely submissions, use of the activity and project costing tools, and forecast reliability.

(c)   QUALITY MEASURES

Adherence to the major practices required to sustain viable activity and project-costing processes should be the major focal point for the quality measures. For example, a process team and owner must be selected to implement improvement opportunities identified by an activity-costing analysis. Further, activity costing becomes an analytical tool that will be marginalized unless action-based budgeting becomes a requirement for supporting annual budget submissions.

14.8   KEY CHALLENGES

The level of effort is fitting given that these two processes are the foundation for the management of the twenty-first century corporation. The major obstacle to the successful implementation of both activity costing and project costing and management is discipline. These processes require a significant up-front investment of time and effort, with the benefits being realized over a long period of time. Therefore, management commitment and support is essential.

The twenty-first century virtual corporation will rely upon business process management. Activity-based management will be the management information, reporting, and analytical foundation. Further, business processes just like projects require project-costing and management tools. Action-based budgeting and the core-processing requirement of activity-based management will be the basis for business process budgeting and forecasting. Process management will be approached from a project management perspective.

CHAPTER 15

Performance Reporting and Management

15.1   INTRODUCTION

In this section of the book, we have been discussing the financial management processes that provide the basic underpinning for the overall management of the business:

- Financial planning and analysis
- Budgeting and forecasting
- Cost and profitability management

As we begin to approach a finance function that is able to spend a significant amount of time supporting management and improving finan-

Exhibit 15-1   Performance Management: Making the Transition to Shareholder Advocate

Goal: High-quality strategic and tactical
Business Decisions

Key: Allowing the shareholder to
Set Business Objectives
Ends debate
on what goals

Finance: Becomes the owner of the
Performance Management process that
Improves Business Performance

cial and business results, we must turn back to a basic question: How effectively will the above processes be utilized in combination to maximize shareholder wealth? The approach we take to measuring and assessing management performance will be critical to a cohesive strategic financial management structure and, in turn, assuring that finance is focused on the maximization of shareholder wealth.

Performance reporting is the next step in the effort to shift the focus of finance from accounting for to managing business results. Exhibit 15-1 reinforces the importance of the shareholder as the primary driver for the transformation of finance.

Performance reporting provides the foundation for high-quality strategic and tactical business decisions:

- *Information:* to manage business and financial performance

- *Perspective and context:*   to assess business and financial performance
- *Capacity:*   to evaluate management performance

15.2   BENCHMARKING

The major goal for finance is to provide value-added analysis and information. Performance reporting and management is central to this transformation. A world-class financial planning and analysis function should spend at least 50 percent of its time on performance modeling and analysis.

15.3   REENGINEERING

To create a world-class performance reporting process, finance must leverage budgeting and forecasting by identifying leading indicators of future results and the key drivers contributing to current-period results.

A major benefit of using performance metrics is the ability to gain insight that can be used to manage results. For instance, customer-satisfaction ratings—ranging from defects to fill rates—provide some sense of what may be bothering them and the likelihood that they will continue to buy from the company. This is very important information to assure customer retention and maintain a market image that will attract new customers.

Most companies can measure all the right things, but they are not seeing the expected benefits. The problem is that the measurements have become the focal point to evaluating management performance. Rather than being seen as a means to an end, performance metrics have become the end point.

The dilemma that has been created by performance metrics is that companies tend to measure management against the performance metric rather than the end that is being sought—sales growth. Management has a wide variety of options and constraints that must be managed within an integrated operating framework to achieve the ultimate results that the shareholder is looking for:

- Sales growth
- Profitability growth
- Initiatives that will provide the capabilities to maximize long-term shareholder wealth

Performance metrics are the levers that management can use to assess and manage business performance to meet shareholder requirements. When the metrics become the focal point of management evaluation, there is a major disconnect when managers meet their performance goals but not the shareholder goals. There are two major questions:

1. Is it assumed that if all the right things are done, the shareholder requirements will be met?
2. Is it assumed that if management is held accountable for meeting shareholder requirements, the right things will be managed to get the results expected?

The answer to both questions should be yes.

First, senior management reporting to the president or chair of the board of directors must be held accountable for meeting shareholder requirements—as discussed in chapter 13, Budgeting and Forecasting (see exhibits 15-2 and 15-3). It does not matter whether customer sat-

Exhibit 15-2   What Are the Commitments?

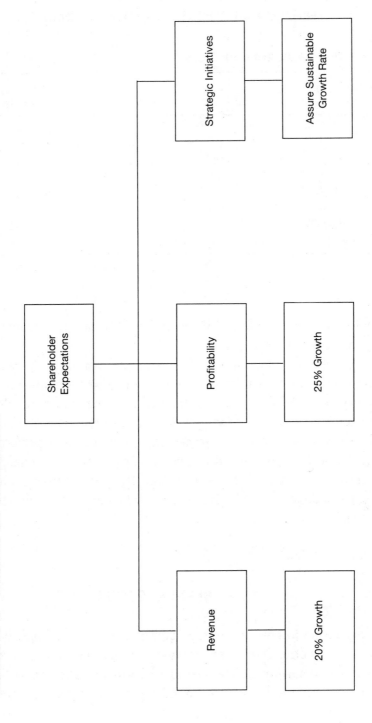

Exhibit 15-3   Key Areas of Focus

Responsibility Area	Revenue	Profitability	Strategic Initiatives
Sales	Sales force efficiency	Sales force effectiveness	Strategic alliances
Marketing	New product	Pricing	Five-year product plan
Operations	Schedule compliance	Rework	Technology
Customer service	Customer satisfaction	Technical training	Outsourcing

isfaction has been improved if the expected benefits in financial performance are not achieved.

While performance metrics will provide insight, they cannot be used to measure management performance. Managers must not have any way to deflect their accountability for meeting shareholder requirements. If sales go down but customer satisfaction goes up, and both are equally considered in assessing management performance, what should be done? From a shareholder perspective, management did not meet its requirements. However, from an internal evaluation, the job was done half right. Half right offers management an opportunity to say it did its job.

15.4   BEST PRACTICES

The discipline to convert strategy and budgets into management actions requires clear thinking about how competitive advantage will ultimately be determined. The use of performance metrics to link the key aspects of competitiveness to the basic management processes of the business helps lay the groundwork for developing the road map to accomplishing the strategy.

Performance measurements come into play by assuring that there are attributes available to measure progress. Without any means of evaluating forward movement, companies are basically managing in the dark. Keep in mind that business strategy has expectations and, therefore, attributes that can be monitored. Because performance measures are based on planned actions required to accomplish strategy, the process of determining the right measures may point out flaws in the plans.

Exhibit 15-4 shows how performance measures must be built on planned actions and the expected benefits or results associated with each action. Performance metrics are built to measure and monitor the actions and associated results. (See exhibit 15-5.) Measurements that are not directly linked to planned actions serve to distract and add complexity when evaluating results. Further, they demonstrate a lack

Exhibit 15-4   What We Need to Accomplish

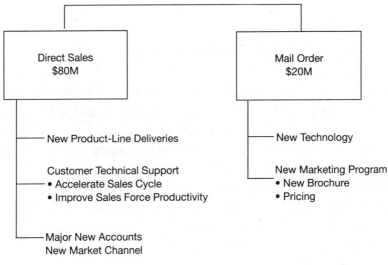

Exhibit 15-5   Are We Delivering the Results?

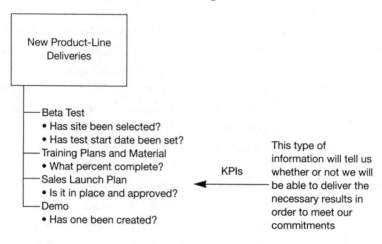

of understanding of how day-to-day management can be directed by business plans.

15.5   IMPLEMENTATION

By leading the effort to develop an integrated performance model, finance will begin to understand all the key drivers and levers of business and management performance. In addition, the performance model will provide a clear demonstration of finance's business insight and commitment to business partnership.

The first step is to break down budget commitments by the actions designed to achieve those commitments. There is one rule: The financial results of major actions or initiatives must in total equal the budget commitments made to the shareholders.

15.6 REENGINEERED PROCESS FLOW

Performance reporting and management integrates the major strategic financial planning processes that focus on improving financial and business performance. In essence, this process is intended to be a conceptual model that focuses the strategic financial management processes on the right things.

The previous chapters have attempted to emphasize the right things, but it is important to reinforce the need for providing an analytical and strategic framework that will provide finance with the direction and tools to become business partners.

Performance management is dependent on following best practices for each of the strategic financial management processes:

- Financial planning and analysis
- Budgeting and forecasting
- Cost and performance management
- Shareholder and treasury management processes, discussed in the next section

15.7 MEASURING PERFORMANCE

Measuring the performance of this process should be approached from the view of conducting an exam of the health of the overall finance function. The performance measures should focus on finance's performance in these critical mission areas:

- Business partnership
- Shareholder advocate

- Technology infrastructure and tools to deliver timely, value-added services
- Organizational and process capabilities to improve business and financial performance and maximize shareholder wealth

Exhibit 15-6 is the beginning of an ongoing effort to determine the performance attributes that exemplify the essence of a world-class financial organization.

In the earlier exhibits the final results of this effort were highlighted. Here, it is necessary to begin with the fundamentals, identifying the levers or drivers that must be influenced to achieve management commitments.

The following three exhibits (15-7, 15-8, and 15-9) walk through the process of linking budget commitments to actions that can be measured and monitored. First, sales management's targets are looked at as a way to emphasize that dollar commitments can be assigned in absolute terms. All senior executive commitments, in total, meet the company's commitment to the shareholders. Second, the first level of levers influencing revenue growth is identified. Third, factors that must be addressed to effectively manage these levers to achieve management commitments are examined. This drill-down process points to the opportunity that revenue growth can be modeled and performance measured.

15.8   KEY CHALLENGES

The use of performance metrics has often been relegated to analytical tool kits rather than a strategic tool integrating the efforts of finance to maximize shareholder wealth.

Traditionally, performance reporting management has been

Exhibit 15-6 Performance Reporting and Management: Performance Measures

---

Business Partnership
Finance counsel actively sought out
Finance often leading major business initiatives
Finance a major source of profitability improvements and new business
  opportunities

Shareholder Advocate
Management and employees recognize the importance of meeting
  shareholder expectations
Operating budget is linked to shareholder requirements
Departmental budgets can be related to shareholder requirements

Technology Infrastructure and Tools
Integrated financial and operating systems
Common data architecture
Real-time recognition of financial and business information
Information that is easily accessible with appropriate levels of security
Decision support tools that are easy to use and have robust capabilities

Organizational and Process
Line and non-finance functional assignments are critical elements of finance's
  organizational development strategy
Finance experience seen as valuable for senior staff and line executive
  promotions
Finance organization is seen as lean and cost effective
Financial processes are streamlined minimizing administrative work
Strategic financial management processes contribute to management's
  ability to improve financial and business performance

---

more than a measure created by using the skills and tool kit of activity-based costing and management. Therefore, the analytical preoccupation and novelty of performance measures has not been justified and has only diminished its potential, relegating this concept to the closet of analytical tools that are excellent but seldom used. Further, the analytical haughtiness of people attempting to de-

Exhibit 15-7   Sales Management—Performance/Improvement/Drill-Down

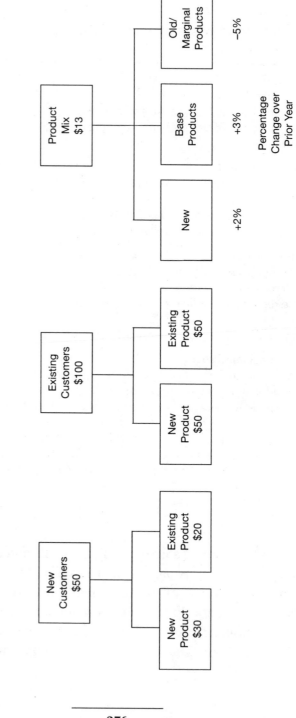

Revenue Growth ($ millions)

Profitability

New Customers $50
— New Product $30
— Existing Product $20

Existing Customers $100
— New Product $50
— Existing Product $50

Product Mix $13
— New   +2%
— Base Products   +3%
— Old/Marginal Products   −5%

Percentage Change over Prior Year

Exhibit 15-8 Revenue Growth

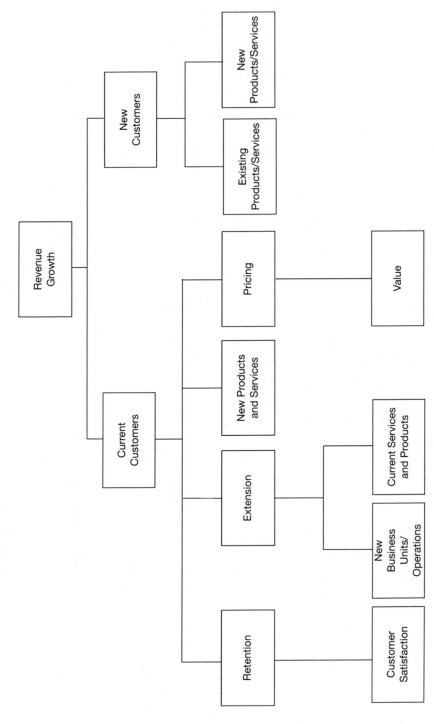

Exhibit 15-9 Revenue Growth

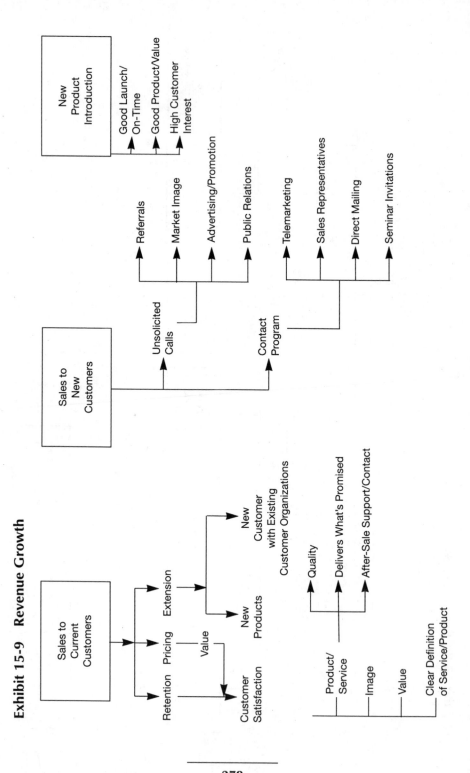

velop key performance indicators has created an allure of analytical sophistication that (1) is not merited and (2) scares people from using it.

To be effective and valuable, performance measurements should be based on common-sense analysis of what drives business results, tagging information generated from the normal course of business to track action plans and results.

CHAPTER 16

Cash and Working Capital Management

16.1 INTRODUCTION

Cash is the lifeblood of a business and a key driver of shareholder value. From a shareholder perspective, cash flow is the funding source for dividends and an indicator of a company's ability to cover fixed cost.

An analysis of cash flow from the sources and uses of funds statement is an excellent summary of the financial health of a business. There are two categories that generate the majority of the sources and uses of funds. They are:

Sources of Funds from Operations	Use of Funds from Operations
Operations:	
Operating Profits	Capital Expenditures
Noncash Expenses	Prepaid Expenses
Financial:	
Change in Working Capital	Change in Working Capital
Increase in Long-Term Debt	Repayment of Debt
Equity	Dividends
Retained Earnings	Stock Buybacks

Given that the sources and uses of funds from operations are a given, the question is how can treasury optimize the sources and uses of funds under its control:

- In the short term the focus is liquidity, which includes working capital management and managing cash position.
- The long-term focus is capital structure, which includes corporate financing and managing the cost of debt and the cost of capital.

16.2   BENCHMARKING

Benchmarking the cost of cash management should include all banking fees. Cost per dollar should be used to compare cost [total cost/(total receipts + total disbursements)].

16.3   REENGINEERING

Cash management is the operations side and working capital management is the planning side of managing the liquidity of a company.

16.3 Reengineering

The major objective of working capital management is to plan and forecast the cash requirements of the business to allow cash management to anticipate cash needs. Planning and forecasting is essential in order to anticipate the maximum lines of credit needed to cover short-term cash needs.

When a company's working capital and cash requirements cannot be forecasted, the company's cost of debt will increase accordingly:

- Reducing financial leverage
- Increasing financing cost

Financial leverage is hurt because a company is forced to more conservatively manage working capital. Finance must be more conservative to protect liquidity:

- When cash is available to long-term initiatives, management will be reluctant to take advantage of the positive short-term funds position to finance longer-term projects.
- When cash is tight, management will be more conservative in its use of long-term capital, by holding a higher level in reserve to cover short-term financial needs.

Devoting a higher percentage of financial resources for financing operations will limit a company's ability to:

- Invest in its future
- Leverage shareholders' equity
- Increase dividends or stock repurchases

Larger lines of credit to assure adequate liquidity lead to higher financing cost due to:

- Incremental cost for obtaining commitments for larger lines of credit
- Higher interest rate charges for credit risk

By recognizing the downside of poor working capital management, one can appreciate the financial leverage that can be realized by strong working capital management. Strong working capital management requires a disciplined and accurate operating and capital forecast. (The requirements for a good operating forecast were discussed in chapter 13, Budgeting and Forecasting. The requirements for a good capital budget will be discussed in chapter 18, Corporate Finance.)

The major issues for working capital management are:

- Changes to working capital from the operating forecast
  - inventory
  - accounts receivable
  - accounts payable
- Impact of capital project forecast on cash and working capital
  - current-period cash requirements
  - future commitments that will create future-period liabilities
  - status against plan that will gauge level of forecast risk or reliability
- Impact of corporate finance plans on working capital
  - sources of funds from new equity or debt
  - uses of funds for dividends, stock repurchases, and repayment of debt

16.4 BEST PRACTICES

Strong planning and forecasting and consolidation of financial operations and banks are essential to creating a world-class cash and working capital management process. Best practices related to these requirements include:

Banking Relationships
- One to two primary banks
- Automated polling of banks
- Systematic polling of balances during day
- Analysis of fee versus compensating balance cost
- Reliable operating forecast to determine short-term cash needs

Financial Operations
- Access to payable and receivable systems to forecast weekly and daily cash requirements
- Controlled disbursements through EDI
- Purchasing cards

Planning/Forecasting
- Disciplined capital budgeting
- Reliable forecasting
- Visibility to future purchasing and sales commitments

16.5   IMPLEMENTATION

There are a number of options available to cash management to improve cash position and reduce financing cost. There are four actions by which cash management can improve cash position and reduce financing cost:

1. Consolidating banks
2. Centralizing financial transactions

3. Implementing a purchasing card program
4. Improving forecasting reliability

(a) BANK CONSOLIDATION

Bank consolidation gives larger companies the ability to negotiate bank fees and the amount of compensating balances. Using fewer banks improves treasury's ability to focus on managing cash during the day. Further, by concentrating cash into a single bank, treasury minimizes the percentage swings in cash balances and better coordinates cash disbursements with anticipated cash receipts.

(b) CENTRALIZATION OF FINANCIAL TRANSACTION SYSTEMS

The value of centralization is that it improves treasury's visibility to all financial transaction information. In large companies with stand-alone financial transaction systems at each operating location, treasury will normally have limited access to the information in these systems. With limited visibility to financial information, cash management cannot accurately forecast short-term cash requirements. Unable to forecast cash requirements, cash management is then forced to react to daily cash activity.

This results in cash management always funding yesterday's cash position. Unable to forecast requirements, cash management has to wait for the final daily cash position before determining whether to draw down on lines of credit or to place excess cash in short-term securities to increase interest income. One of the leaders in cash management is able to forecast its daily and weekly cash requirements. The accuracy of this company's cash forecast allows it to take actions to invest or draw down on lines of credit during the day rather than waiting for receipt of the end-of-the-day cash positions. The value is that the forecast enables cash management to proactively manage its cash position, minimizing borrowing cost and maximizing interest income on cash exceeding short-term requirements.

(c) PURCHASING CARDS

Of all the tools available to the cash manager, full-scale implementation of purchasing cards offers the greatest opportunities to optimize cash position.

For purchases, a company can increase its days outstanding beyond thirty days, since the credit card payments are not normally due until twenty-five days after the statement date. Assuming spending is relatively stable across the statement period, the average number of days purchases outstanding for the statement is fifteen—allowing accounts payable to be extended to forty days outstanding.

Credit card transactions for sales can significantly reduce days sales outstanding below thirty days. Typically, a company will receive cash payment in as few as one to three working days after the sales transaction—an opportunity to reduce days sales outstanding by as many as twenty-nine days. Given the above assumption, what impact would this have on a $100 million company? Assuming that all purchases were made on a credit card, purchase cost equaled 45 percent of sales, and sales and purchasing were even across all months of the year, credit cards would have the following impact on cash position:

	Total	Days Outstanding		
		Standard	Credit Card	Cash Impact
Monthly Sales	$8.3 million	30 days $8.3 million	3 days $860,000	27 days +$7.4 million
Monthly Purchases	$3.4 million	30 days $3.4 million	45 days $5.1 million	15 days +$1.7 million

Reduction in days sales outstanding reduces a company's debt requirements by $7.4 million that would be required to finance customer receivables. Increase in days purchases outstanding reduces a company's debt requirements by $1.7 million that would be required to finance purchases. A $9.1 million reduction in working capital financing requirements would reduce financing cost and reduce the lines of credit or the amount of permanent working capital financing.

Besides improving cash position, credit card purchases and sales will significantly improve cash forecasting. For purchases, the payment due date is constant throughout the year. Given that the amount and due date for credit card purchases are reported on the monthly statement, cash management can plan two to four weeks in advance the case requirements for these purchases.

For sales, the timing of cash receipts from the date of purchase and the associated discount is fixed. Therefore, the only variable is the sales forecast. The more accurate the sales forecast, the more accurately cash management will be able to predict cash receipts. Further, credit or economic factors that could adversely impact cash receipts from outstanding credit would be eliminated by the use of credit cards.

(d) BUDGETING AND FORECASTING RELIABILITY

The financial impact from improving budgeting and forecasting must become visible. This will require the active monitoring of cash and working capital budget and forecasting reliability in tandem with capital and operating budgets and forecast. This should include the cost of extra lines of credit required to compensate for unexpected cash requirements.

16.6   REENGINEERED PROCESS FLOW

The reengineered process flow in exhibit 16-1 emphasizes:

- The need for good planning
- The importance of a good cash management
- The benefits of integrated financial operating systems that provide total visibility to the working capital and cash disbursements/receipts

16.7   MEASURING PERFORMANCE

The performance measures for cash and working capital management emphasize the importance of forecast reliability. (See exhibit 16-2.)

(a)   COST DRIVERS

The two major drivers of non-value-added time and cost are:

1. Limited visibility to pending financial transactions and bank account cash activities during the day
2. Reliability and confidence in the integrity of capital and operating budgets and forecasts

Exhibit 16-1 Cash and Working Capital Management Process

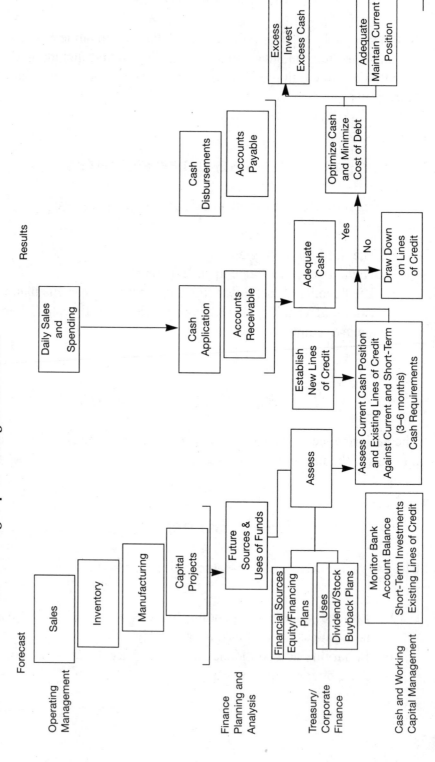

**Exhibit 16-2   Cost and Working Capital Management
Performance Measures**

Cost Drivers
Decentralized financial and business systems
Number of banks and accounts
Integrity of capital budgeting and management
Reliable operation budgets and forecasts

Productivity Measures
Percent of time responding to unanticipated changes in cash and
   working capital positions
Dollar amount and cost of unused lines of credit
Dollar value and cost to secure emergency lines of credit
Percent of sales and purchase transaction using purchasing credit cards

Quality Measures
Minimizing cost of debt
Meeting immediate and interest rate short-term funding requirements
Forecast reliability

(b)   PRODUCTIVITY MEASURES

Predictability is the critical element to improving productivity and
lowering the cost of cash management. Therefore, the productivity
metrics focus on:

- Cost and time to react to unanticipated cash and working capital requirements
- Increasing the percentage of purchasing card transactions
- Reducing working capital requirements
- Increasing predictability of cash requirements

(c)   QUALITY MEASURES

The ultimate measure of quality is improving business results by:

- Minimizing financing cost
- Meeting the funding requirements of the business when needed

16.8   KEY CHALLENGES

Forecast reliability and access to financial transaction and business systems are the key to creating a world-class cash management process. This will require a greater emphasis on the accuracy of working capital forecasting. The importance of a good financial operations environment requires that cash management must work closely with financial operations management.

Finally, cash and working capital management performance is an excellent performance measure for the integrity of the financial transaction processes and the budgeting and forecasting processes. To reinforce the benefits of improving these financial processes, cash and working capital management must identify the improvement to financing cost and accessibility to funding that they can achieve by managing world-class financial transaction and budgeting/forecasting processes.

CHAPTER 17

Investor Relations

17.1 INTRODUCTION

Investor relations is fundamentally a communications process. Both form and substance are important.

The form of communications must be open and honest. This requires an ongoing dialogue with the investment community and a regular program of meeting with major shareholders.

To accomplish this open and honest dialogue will require that management be able to present a clear picture of the company's current and future direction. All investors attempt to manage risk within the framework of their investment strategy. A major factor in their risk equation is the amount of open and honest communication from management. Given the presentation of the same set of facts, the level of shareholders' confidence in the company's plans and the integrity of management will amplify up or down an investor's risk assessment of a company.

17.2 BENCHMARKING

Improvements to market value and rate of return on shareholder value are the benchmarks to measure investor relations.

17.3 REENGINEERING

Understanding the investment goals of the shareholders is essential to the effectiveness of investor relations. The targets that management must set to maximize shareholder wealth will be influenced by the shareholders. Shareholder goals can be grouped into three major categories:

- Income
- Income and growth
- Growth

This investment view is common among the majority of mutual funds, which characterize their funds into similar groupings. This allows fund managers to define their investment strategies in terms that allow investors to match their investment goals to the appropriate funds. The fund managers then spend their time looking for companies that fit into their investment strategy.

The mutual fund industry's growth is due in large part to the fact that investors are able to make investment decisions based on their investment goals. The focus then shifts to which funds' bases perform within each investment classification. Considering the investment criteria of the shareholders should not be limited to mutual fund managers. Companies must understand the ownership class of their share-holders to optimize the key drivers of shareholder wealth to meet and exceed their shareholders' requirements.

The following chart highlights how ownership class will influence the requirements for the key drivers of shareholder wealth. This analysis focuses on the relative importance of the key drivers to the specific ownership class. With a baseline that all drivers of shareholder wealth are equal in importance, an analysis can be made of the relative importance by ordinal ranking that shareholders might place on these drivers within each ownership class.

	Ranking of Drivers by Ownership Class		
Key Drivers	*Income*	*Income and Growth*	*Growth*
Confidence/ Future Plans	5	3	1
Operating Results	1	1	5
Liquidity	2	2	3
Capital Structure	3	4	2
Risk	4	5	4

By considering the relative importance of a driver to an owner, one can begin a process of helping to define shareholder requirements and evaluate trade-offs.

17.4   BEST PRACTICES

Best practices in investor relations focus on reliable and open communications.

- Proactively managing analyst expectations and evaluation of management and company performance

- Strategically managing rating agencies and investment community
  - clear business and financial information to evaluate management and current business condition
  - coherent proactive view of company plans to build market expectations
  - management's preparation and support to prevent surprises and to address all analysts' questions
- Building strong relationship with analysts
  - easily accessible, responsive
  - reliable information
- Rating agency and investment community meetings that provide analysts with the information required and management presentations that support results in all answers
- Providing internal management with clear understanding of investment community
  - view of the company
  - requirements for increasing market valuation and access to financing
- Coordinating/assuring that there is a common message

17.5   IMPLEMENTATION

A successful reengineering program for investor relations must begin with management recognition of the positive effects that investor relations can have on shareholder value.

People have a tendency to be somewhat conservative when receiving management forecasts. The more uncomfortable they are with the integrity and reliability of the management team, the more they will adjust downward its estimates. Lack of confidence in management has a tremendous impact on how the price/earnings ratio impacts market value:

- The ratio will tend to be lower than the industry average.
- Lower earning estimates result directly in a lower market value.

Consider a company with fifty thousand shares of stock.

- The industry price/earnings ratio is eight; however, because of the lack of confidence in the company and management, the ratio is six.
- Further, management's forecast of $5.00/share is adjusted downward by the markets to $3.50.

Based on the industry standard, the market valuation of the company would be $20 million. However, this company's market valuation will be only $10.5 million. The cost to the shareholders is $9.5 million.

If the true forecast were in fact $3.50 and management communications were reliable, then the price/earnings ratio would increase to either seven or eight:

- A ratio of seven would result in a market value of $12.2 million—a $1.7 million increase.
- A ratio of eight would result in a market value of $14 million—a $3.5 million increase.

In other words, it is better to tell the market the truth, no matter how bad it is; otherwise, the market will make the corrections on its own and penalize the company in the process.

Embedded in the form is the substance of what is being communicated. Substance obviously impacts form because its quality and reliability are directly related to open and honest communications.

Further, the quality and insight of the substance of the business plans and management insight will influence the market's perception of the competence of management.

All of the above can be summed up in the market's confidence in management. Confidence in management will dictate market value more than any other single variable. Consider what happens when a successful turnaround executive comes into a struggling company. Immediately the market begins to increase its assessment of the value of the company. As that executive begins to demonstrate results, the market valuation will benefit.

(a) SHAREHOLDER INVESTMENT CRITERIA

While shareholders' investment criteria may differ (investor-risk return tradeoff versus owner-income versus capital appreciation), the common denominator is the same: return versus risk. Using the above or another set of performance criteria, investor relations managers meet with shareholders and key members of the financial community to understand exactly what the investment goals are for their company. While industry groups will tend to gravitate toward a particular ownership class, this still needs to be clarified and turned into tangible performance criteria.

This process must actively engage the shareholders in setting the priorities for the company. Once these priorities are set, management has a baseline and framework to build a business plan. Results will then be reported in a manner that will help the board and shareholders assess how business performance will impact their investments.

Investor relations must work also with the shareholders and board to establish the performance criteria for the key drivers of shareholder wealth. Communication of shareholder and financial market requirements and expectations to management and the employees must become a major and recurring activity for investor relations.

As discussed earlier in this chapter, the closer an organization can feel and relate to the owners, the more likely the organization will instill the attitude that all employees have financial and management responsibilities that contribute to the success of the business and the owners.

(b)   BUSINESS PLANS

The business plans reflect the capabilities of management and the long-term potential of the company. While this book will not get into an extensive discussion of the planning process, it is important to emphasize that the business plan must take into consideration the shareholders' investment criteria and recognize that plans for the future will require the use of shareholder capital. No money is free.

Recognizing that the business is dependent on the retention of shareholders' capital, the business plan should begin with the shareholders' investment criteria. Based on the shareholder performance requirements, management should prepare a business plan addressing:

- Business outlook and strategy
- Details of the timing of actions and their associated investment and operating costs
- Tangible results and benefits with associated attributes that can be used to measure performance

Shareholders should be able to assess the plan and its expected outcomes against the key drivers of shareholder wealth:

- *Operating results:*   current- and future-period profitability
- *Liquidity:*   cash flow to finance operations and cover dividends
- *Capital structure:*   financial leverage and return on equity
- *Risk:*   financial/economic risk; competitive/technology risk; product/regulatory/casualty

The plan should be structured to differentiate the core business requirements from new business initiatives. Beginning with a baseline plan for the core business, the plan should assess whether the core business is able to meet shareholder requirements. If the answer is no, then the option of liquidation or sale of the company should be considered. The shareholders should not be subsidizing the business by accepting a lower rate of return.

Each major business initiative should be addressed in a similar fashion but should also identify the incremental capital (debt and equity) and cash flow impact. While capital budgeting will be expanded upon in chapter 18, Corporate Finance, the major point is that each major business initiative should be viewed from the perspective of shareholders' capital allocation model. If we cannot meet the criteria, then the shareholders' capital should be returned to the shareholders through dividends.

17.6   REENGINEERED PROCESS FLOW

The reengineered process flow for investor relations emphasizes active involvement with both the financial community and the company (see exhibit 17-1). Linking shareholder requirements with

Exhibit 17-1 Investor Relations Process Flow

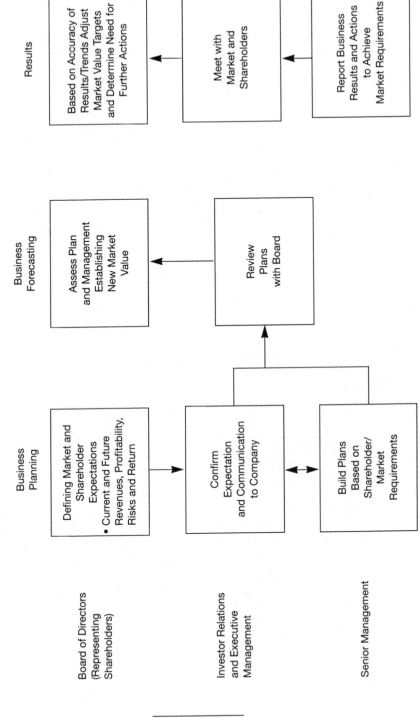

management commitments is the driving force that moves this process.

17.7 MEASURING PERFORMANCE

The performance measures in exhibit 17-2 emphasize the level and reliability of communications with the shareholders and the financial markets. Confidence in management and the company's future are levers that can significantly and immediately improve market value.

Exhibit 17-2 Performance Measures: Investor Relations

Cost Drivers
Unpredictable financial performance
Poor financial performance
Return to shareholders below expectations
Disgruntled shareholders
Number of shareholders
Number of analyst presentations and shareholder meetings

Productivity Measures
Time to prepare for presentations and shareholder meetings
Response time to information request from shareholders, analyst

Quality Measures
Consistency and accuracy of responses to analysts
Rating agency/analyst presentations
Analyst/market confidence in management
Annual report
Accuracy of forecast

17.8   KEY CHALLENGES

The key challenge facing investor relations is the recognition that its managers are serving as the voice of the shareholder. Further, the more shareholder expectations are planned for and met, the greater the increase in market value beyond the current and projected financial results.

CHAPTER 18

Corporate Finance

18.1 INTRODUCTION

The corporate finance function's major objective is optimizing the cost of capital to meet the shareholders' expectations for return on capital invested or return on shareholder value.

To meet this objective, corporate finance must be able to communicate:

- For business planning purposes the business results needed to meet shareholders' expected rate of return on their investment—whether return on equity or return on market value
- For capital budgeting, establishing decision criteria for return on investment

Given the predominance of market value in shareholder return requirements, the impact of financing and capital spending decisions should be expanded to consider impact on shareholder wealth.

To assure the company is able to meet shareholders' expectations, corporate finance must then develop a capital structure plan addressing: (1) accessibility and forms of financing, (2) management of cost of debt to meet shareholder return requirements, and (3) consideration of the impact on market value or future market value (shareholder wealth) from strategic investments.

18.2   REENGINEERING

From the viewpoint of the shareholder, one dilemma that corporate finance must address is whether to use the cost of capital or the shareholders' expected rate of returns for corporate investment. In most cases, the cost of capital and the cost of equity will be below shareholders' expected rate of return. Therefore, starting with the cost of capital rate as the base from which to evaluate returns on capital investment leads to investments that will not meet shareholders' expected rate of returns. The cost of shareholders' capital against alternative uses of their capital should be the starting point for developing the hurdle rate for business and capital investments. A shortcut to addressing this problem is to treat cost of debt as an operating expense when measuring a company's or investment's ability to meet shareholder expected rate of return. To the extent that treasury enhances the financial leverage of shareholders' capital, this should be viewed as a key element in the income statement for both budgeting and long-range planning and not a factor to be incorporated into the company's hurdle rates for capital investments.

The execution of corporate finance's capital management responsibilities hinges on the effectiveness of the capital budgeting process. Capital budgeting should assume that capital spending will be financed by shareholder capital. How spending is actually funded is the responsibility of treasury. However, treasury should identify all financing sources for the planning period and how those resources will be put to use. This would require that earnings retained by the company must identify their dollar amount and primary purposes, such as capital spending or working capital. If a single initiative will require more than 25 percent of that financing category spending or 10 percent of total planned financing, the project should be identified. These percentages are used to suggest the level of spending that would be material to a company. For your company, the percentages might be higher or lower.

Although capital spending will assume the use of shareholders' capital and must meet their expected rate of returns, the reality is that the cost and access to debt financing will be a major influence on capital spending's total year authorization level. Treasury should address how the cost and access to debt and shareholders' capital impacts:

- The amount of funding available for capital investments
- Operating profitability and expected income contributions from capital spending, thereby assuring that changes to fixed cost and financing cost will be factors considered in determining how total capital spending will influence profitability and long-term fixed-cost structure

By addressing the factors that help set the capital spending authorization level, this section aims to emphasize that resources are limited and prioritization of spending decisions is necessary. Capital decisions confirm business priorities and requirements:

- Operational and strategic priorities
  - product development
  - maintenance and infrastructure improvements
  - major reengineering initiatives
  - plant and equipment
  - acquisitions
- Requirements
  - return on shareholder value
  - discipline and commitment to deliver results
  - program leadership accountability

Establishing priorities will require that the merits of each project be weighed against the merits of all other proposed projects under consideration. Further, if a project is not in the business plans it cannot be taken under consideration, which in most cases will result in it not being funded during the current year.

This will encourage people to plan ahead so that their projects will receive authorization. By prioritizing projects against one another, management must focus attention on monitoring project results against plan. Post-project review will be necessary to help management address to what extent submissions from individuals or organizations can be relied upon. A person whose projects always meet profit and performance forecast will provide management and the investment committee with a high level of confidence that a current proposal's forecasted improvements will be realized. Conversely, an individual whose projects are always below forecasted results will give management little confidence that the current proposal will deliver the results projected. We are creating track records that can be used for assessing project risk.

Now that a clear set of guidelines for optimizing long-term capital structure and current-period working capital has been laid out, the focus shifts to planning and managing investment decisions.

18.3 BEST PRACTICES

An accurate forecast of capital needs allows corporate finance to optimize the capital structure and anticipate funding requirements to take advantage of timing to reduce the cost of debt and minimize the amount of credit lines for unexpected cash or capital needs.

Accurate forecasting is dependent on the quality of the capital budgeting and business investment planning process. The following are the best practices of this process:

- Three-year project pipeline
- Preliminary design and evaluation completed prior to budget
- Budget final approval for all projects
- Maintenance planning is an integral component of capital planning
- Continuous investment management process (eighteen to twenty-four months out)
- Strategic/financial prioritization
- Simple/fast/consistent method of screening, approval, and authorization
- Visible program status and results
- Early identification of investment needs and opportunities
- Project specifications and cost estimates complete prior to budgeting

18.4 IMPLEMENTATION

(a) CAPITAL BUDGETING AND BUSINESS INVESTMENT PLANNING

Optimization of capital structure requires a disciplined capital budgeting and business investment planning process. This book adds business investment planning to emphasize the necessity for disciplined long-range planning.

The major benefits of implementing a comprehensive approach to managing capital investments include:

- *Strategic:* connecting point between business strategy and required capital investments
- *Tactical:* clearinghouse for capital spending requests to be prioritized spending and to ferret out initiatives that are inconsistent with the business plans and a drain on management time and resources
- *Transformation:* establishing an environment that holds people accountable for results

The capital budgeting and business investment process offers finance an opportunity to instill a deliberative process for planning capital spending requirements and a disciplined project management throughout the entire investment life cycle. This approach to capital spending will improve treasury's ability to manage:

- Long-term capital structure
- Midterm working capital requirements
- Current- and short-term liquidity and cash requirements

This approach requires management leaders with:

- Foresight to plan for the future
- Ability to execute their responsibilities to achieve their planning commitments

This process touches on the core requirement for transforming the business enterprise into the twenty-first century virtual corporation—

empowerment. This empowerment aligns the responsibility for taking action with the accountability for delivering results from the beginning of an initiative to its completion.

Capital budgeting and business investment process must relate empowerment to management leadership. By empowering leaders to lead, treasury is then in a position to plan and manage financing and capital structure issues with confidence that the business plans will be executed and will meet management expectations.

(b)   CAPITAL BUDGETING AND BUSINESS INVESTMENT PLANNING LIFE CYCLE

Capital budgeting and business investment planning is a three- to five-year process that is structured to manage the life cycle of a capital spending initiative:

Life Cycle Phase	Time Before Project Start Date	Decision or Action Required
Long-Range Plan	3–5 years	Concept approval
Program Approval	18–30 months	Proof of concept and preliminary design
Capital Budget	12–18 months	Engineered and detailed project schedule
Project Management	6–18 months	Compliance with schedule and spending
Performance Review	+2 months	Assess financial and business performance

The above time line is for major capital projects. Since *major* is a relative term, we should consider using 10 percent of total capital spending as the trigger for requiring that a project go through the above process. To prevent establishing multiple projects to stay under the 10 percent level, the 10 percent rule should be applied to all capital spending. This will require that all capital spending projects fall into one of three categories:

- Individual project
- Grouping of related projects
- Miscellaneous projects

By requiring that unrelated projects must be identified as a group, all projects will see the light of day, which will prevent efforts to hide major projects by dividing them so that they are under the threshold.

(c) COORDINATION

The capital budgeting and business investment process must be coordinated by a management committee made up of representatives of all major line and functional organizations. This committee is responsible for managing the process and approving capital spending for each phase of the life cycle. Its responsibility is to screen projects to assure:

- Spending meets investor rate of return requirements
- Project is consistent with business plans and strategy
- Disciplined project management

While this committee will have responsibility for authorizing projects to proceed to the next stage, senior management and the board of directors ultimately have final approval of projects. This approval takes place through the long-range planning and the capital budgeting process, where major capital spending initiatives will be high-lighted.

By handling corporate approval of major projects through both the long-range plan and capital budget, the board and senior management can evaluate the project on its merits and consistency with the strategic direction of the business. Their ability to focus on the value and benefit of the capital spending initiatives is due to the capital budgeting and business investment planning process emphasis on project justification and accurate projections of time, resources, and results processes.

(d)   LONG-RANGE PLAN

All major capital spending requirements must be addressed during the development of the long-range planning process. This plan normally has a time horizon of three to five years and in some companies as far out as ten years. Given the push to compress cycle times for product development, six to nine months in the electronics industry and two to three years in the automotive industry, one could argue that the short product development cycle time prevents planning capital spending three to five years in advance.

While the long-range plan will far exceed the time horizons of most product development or any other major spending project, the need for a conceptual framework for the future will encourage management to identify needs or strategies that will require capital spending.

The long-range plan will assure capital projects are consistent with future business requirements and allow treasury to address the long-term capital structure implications of future investments.

Shareholder wealth, or the future increase in market valuation, should be a central element of the long-range planning process. This will provide a decision to level the playing field for all investment requirements. The name of the capital budgeting process was specifically expanded to include business investments. This addresses funding requirements for projects that could significantly improve shareholder wealth but are not product-related or a capitalizable asset and are therefore excluded from capital funding. These projects are then forced to compete for resources needed to manage today's business.

Shareholder wealth also provides a strategic framework to discuss the relative contribution of projects and initiatives. This will help to neutralize overoptimistic planning by forcing projects to be evaluated on fundamental soundness of the investment.

The major objectives for this first phase of the capital project life cycle are:

- Linking capital spending to the strategic plan—business and financial requirements and impact on shareholder wealth
- Identifying a program champion for major spending initiatives who will have accountability for managing the project and for delivering the expected results
- Conditional authorization of spending and timing that will be dependent upon concept approval that is required prior to program authorization

The long-range plan, combined with investment committee oversight, will help eliminate extraneous pet projects that are a drain on management time and resources.

(e) PROGRAM MANAGEMENT

Once a project concept has been approved, the next step is program management and planning. The major objectives of this phase are:

- Monitoring progress to flag programs that are getting bogged down or where major projections or assumptions have changed
- Preparing preliminary design or conceptual models identifying resource requirements, timing, and expected results
- Completing a due-diligence review validating concept and expected resource requirements and benefits

The program management phase is the most critical step. The skeleton of the capital spending initiative will be defined. Concepts will move from ideas to tangible models or plans by which one can envisions the end results of the spending initiative and how things will change.

(f)   CAPITAL BUDGET

After the program has been completed and approved, the next step is to prepare detailed plans to support funding authorization of the project.

At this point in the process, the objectives, strategic fit, and expected results have been given the support of the investment committee and management. The major objectives of the budget authorization process are to:

- Validate previous assumptions and the viability of the initiative
- Obtain a plan that can track project progress

To help accomplish these objectives, budget authorization requirements will include:

- Completed engineering plans—for product, equipment—or detailed business plans for business initiatives or acquisitions

- Reliable project schedule by quarter
  - percent completion
  - expenditures to date
  - future commitments that cannot be reversed

With a thorough review process in the earlier phases and detailed plans that provide strong support for final approval, a project that is approved as part of the capital budget will require no further approvals. Approval of the budget provides authorization to undertake the project according to the plans submitted to the investment committee and management.

A quarterly forecast of capital spending provides treasury with adequate notice for managing working capital and liquidity. Further, the life cycle approach to capital spending has already given treasury notice of capital funding requirements one to two years in advance of budget authorization.

A major objective of using the budget as authorization is to encourage planning and management accountability. Once the budget is approved, management only has to notify management of material changes that would require a review of the project status to determine if the project should be stopped or moved forward.

By having the detail provided through the budget, management will be able to make better decisions over capital spending reductions in light of any major changes to a company's financial position.

The last major benefit is empowerment and the need for management to be attentive to the progress of capital projects. Authorization to move forward at the time of the budget is partially based on senior management and the investment committee's confidence in the program champion and project team. They are ultimately responsible for the success of the project, and they are also given wide latitude to do their jobs effectively.

This freedom comes with a price—accountability. The program champion and project team have no excuses for failure. There has been adequate planning, and detailed plans and designs were completed prior to authorization. This means that they will have to pay special attention to the plans, because once those plans are approved, the team will be responsible for the results.

This accountability provides management with the confidence necessary to empower the program champion and project team. However, management's ability to hold people responsible and accountable also comes with a price—diligence. An empowered organization requires that management pay attention to results and expected outcomes. There is no gatekeeper approving the project team's actions. Therefore, management must pay attention to the results. To effectively manage an empowered organization on an expected-outcome basis, management must be constantly involved in the day-to-day activities of the business and must have the ability to meet with the project teams on an informal basis to better understand the people and the nature of the projects. This level of involvement will provide management with the necessary insight to evaluate results against plan.

(g) PROJECT MANAGEMENT

With the capital budget authorizing project spending, a strong project management process is essential to assure that management has confidence to authorize projects with the capital budget.

The major requirements for a successful project management process include:

- Conformation of project plans and objectives at the time of the project kickoff—assuring that project commitments are understood and committing the project team to deliver on these commitments
- Project management costing and tracking system to provide the management tools to track and analyze progress and spending
- Integrated financial systems allowing for real-time tracking of project spending

- Weekly project meetings to assure that deadlines are not allowed to slip and problems are addressed immediately
- Proactive communication to keep management and employees aware of project status and expected benefits and to secure their support to solve problems, assuring
  - a fast product launch
  - a rapid learning curve and roll out to new technology or management programs
  - a smooth and quick integration of a business acquisition or merger

This list is intended to reinforce the point that all programs and projects requiring major capital investments should be included in the capital budgeting and business investment process. All major investments are made based on a set of expectations. Successful accomplishment of these expectations requires a plan and major milestones for delivering results. These are the same requirements as for product and plant and equipment investments.

Finally, strong project management requires anticipating and adapting to change. Business and economic conditions can change, and people do make mistakes. Active communications and weekly meetings provide the platform for project management to respond quickly to changing conditions. Management empowerment to act quickly and decisively is based on one condition—that material changes to timing, cost, or expected benefits require senior management review and approval for the project to move forward.

(h) PERFORMANCE REVIEW

One of the biggest weaknesses with managing capital spending is that most companies do not conduct a thorough review of project implementation and expected outcomes.

A disciplined capital planning environment and a long-range plan addressing the growth in market valuation will give corporate financing decisions a very robust analytical foundation to evaluate:

1. Alternative financing strategies to meet funding requirements
2. Alternative equity strategies' impact on market valuation, providing a base for evaluating the impact on shareholder wealth of retaining capital for investment versus the shareholder using the capital to get a better rate of return elsewhere

From an implementation standpoint, the focus of the review will be on project timing, compliance with specifications, and organizational and financial resources. Besides helping companies learn from problems, this review will identify the reliability of management commitments and plans by different project categories.

On an expected outcome basis, the focus is on the expected benefits. Capital decisions are made with the expectation that shareholders will receive an adequate rate of return.

18.5   REENGINEERED PROCESS FLOW

The reengineered process flow in exhibit 18-1 reflects this book's emphasis on the planning and coordination activities that impact the capital requirements and capital structure of the business. The purpose of this chapter is to address the internal processes necessary for supporting a world-class corporate finance. With a strong capital planning and management process combined with an effective investor relations process, corporate finance will have the foundation for developing a plan and strategy for managing capital structure and meeting the shareholders' return on investment criteria.

Exhibit 18-1 Corporate Finance Process Flow

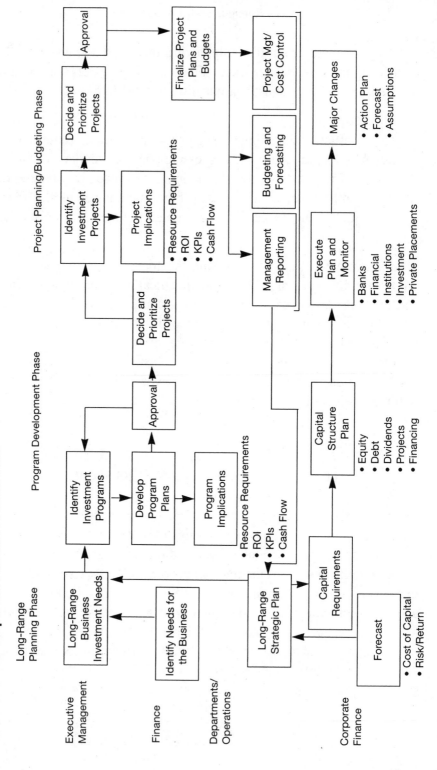

18.6   MEASURING PERFORMANCE

The timely access to capital and reliability of cost of credit/debt forecasts are among the best measures for evaluating the effectiveness of corporate finance. Central to this is a disciplined capital budgeting process that can be best measured by the number of unexpected capital investments. (See exhibit 18-2.)

(a)   COST DRIVERS

Surprises are the major driver of cost for corporate finance. Even if capital spending is reliable, major economic and financial forecast changes can lead to cancellation of financing and delays in issuing equity.

Exhibit 18-2   Performance Measures: Corporate Finance

Cost Drivers
Unexpected capital requirements
Major shifts in interest rates
Mergers, acquisitions, divestitures
Poor financial performance
Return to shareholders below expectations

Productivity Measures
Cycle time for financing
Time to prepare capital forecast and plans
Time to respond to information request

Quality Measures
Time spent with banks and investment community
Time spent with business unit financial and operating executives
Reliability of capital budget forecast
Accuracy of cost of debt/financing forecast
Market value growth rate versus plan

Cost drivers include:

- Percentage change to actual capital budgets
- Percentage of project spending not included in capital budget
- Major changes in economic and financial market conditions

(b) PRODUCTIVITY MEASURES

Planning is essential to effectiveness. Therefore, productivity measures focus on level and reliability of capital spending forecasts and plans.

- Number of changes to financial markets forecasting assumptions during a year
- Forecast accuracy of timing and value of financial actions

(c) QUALITY MEASURES

Good planning requires engaging key members of management and the financial market. Tracking the level of involvement becomes a leading indicator of forecast integrity.

18.7 KEY CHALLENGES

The allure of working with the financial markets can make managing an effective capital planning and management process boring. Which would you choose: going to New York for a week of meetings with investment bankers and financial institutions or spending a week with operating management and controllers discussing current capital projects and long-range spending plans?

18.7 Key Challenges

The emphasis on hiring high-powered finance MBAs for this function will naturally predispose corporate finance staff to choose to work primarily with investment bankers and the financial community. Therefore, the challenge will be to place highly qualified corporate finance people throughout the corporation to manage the internal capital planning and management process as well as to present these plans to the financial institutions and investors.

CHAPTER 19

Risk Management

19.1 INTRODUCTION

The primary goal of treasury risk management is to protect shareholders' invested capital. This has been primarily an insurance acquisition function focusing on:

- Product liability insurance
- Property and casualty insurance
- General liability

In recent years a lot of attention has been paid to financial risk management because of the notoriety of financial derivatives. While financial risk management has normally been the responsibility of corporate finance, with risk management limited to insurance, their goals are nevertheless the same—protection of shareholders' capital.

The major differences between financial versus insurance risk management are:

- Financial risk is central to the execution of treasury responsibilities.
  - currency and commodity hedging
  - financing decisions among short-term debt, long-term debt, and equity and the financing options within each of these categories
  - credit management—which was addressed in chapter 7, Financial Revenue Process, but often reports to treasury
  - investment options of short-term cash
- Property, casualty, product liability, and general liability are handled as insurance activity to minimize the cost and impact on capital from covering current and future liabilities caused by the actions of management and employees

The major goal of risk management must be to establish a strong sense of management accountability for managing the cost of risk and protecting shareholders' capital.

19.2   REENGINEERING

Managing risk is part of the basic fabric of treasury management. While it is of primary concern in the majority of treasury activities, managing liability risk has not been considered a primary responsibility of line management. Because treasury understands risk, and insurance is a financial instrument, insurance risk management has always been a natural fit for treasury.

While financial risk is a daily management activity of treasury, risk that insurance attempts to cover is not a daily activity of management. Consequently, insurance risk management must conduct annual reviews of the company's liability risk. This review will consider the risk that can be created by:

- New environmental regulations that may for instance, require a company to spend significant money to clean up a toxic dump site
- New legal settlements, such as for silicon breast implants or asbestos
- Employee litigation for discrimination or sexual harassment
- Unknown product defects or customer lawsuits claiming such
- Hazardous conditions in the workplace
- Level of fire and casualty protection and general conditions of facilities

19.3 BEST PRACTICES

Best practices emphasize the need for a comprehensive risk management plan and creating a process that shifts accountability for managing risk to operating management.

- Coordinated comprehensive risk management assessment planning process
  - Property
  - Casualty
  - Liability
  - Environmental

- Business unit accountability for risk
  - Premiums allocated based on risk and insurance requirements
  - Risk KPIs linked to evaluation of management performance

19.4   IMPLEMENTATION

A successful reengineering initiative will create a process that aligns responsibility and accountability for risk to operating management with the ability to influence, control, or manage the areas where there is risk exposure.

Risk and the cost of protecting the company from risk must be clearly stated by insurance risk management during the budgeting process. The level of insurance that is estimated to be needed to protect the company from both financial and all other risk must be identified, and the cost of protecting that risk must be identified by category and by the responsible executives.

In other words, the cost of risk management should be assigned to the executives responsible for the areas at risk. Some form of cost allocation is often done at companies. However, allocations by their nature will be viewed as an arbitrary basis for assigning cost to a department or business unit. Allocations imply that the costs incurred by the company are not directly controllable to the department or unit.

While the term allocation may continue to be used by companies, the methodology must be approached from the same view as the insurer in assigning the cost of risk proportionately to the risk exposure associated with the department or business unit. Assessing risk by department and business unit is only the first step; the key to a successful shift of accountability to risk management is giving management the opportunity to manage the cost of risk.

To shift management of the cost of risk to operating management requires giving management the opportunity to control its cost. The next step in this process is to allow management to self-insure a portion of its liability in order to reduce insurance cost. By giving management an opportunity to improve budget profitability, insurance risk and cost will get some notice.

The next step is to place at risk future profits and the financial position of the business unit based on the actual cost incurred from future claims. Rather than having the cost and balance sheet impact handled at the corporate level, companies must assign the cost and balance sheet impact directly to operating management.

Managing future risk can have a silver lining, by offering management the potential for year-end rebates for areas that had better experience ratings than anticipated and adjusting future-year premiums up and down for all organizations as a result of their experience ratings.

19.5   REENGINEERED PROCESS FLOW

The reengineered process flow in exhibit 19-1 emphasizes the active involvement of operating and financial management in the business units. Risk management is integrating the financial and insurance market trends and requirements with the plans and actions of operating management to develop and manage a comprehensive risk management process.

19.6   MEASURING PERFORMANCE

Performance measurements in exhibit 19-2 focus on change and claim activity.

Exhibit 19-1   Risk Management Process Flow

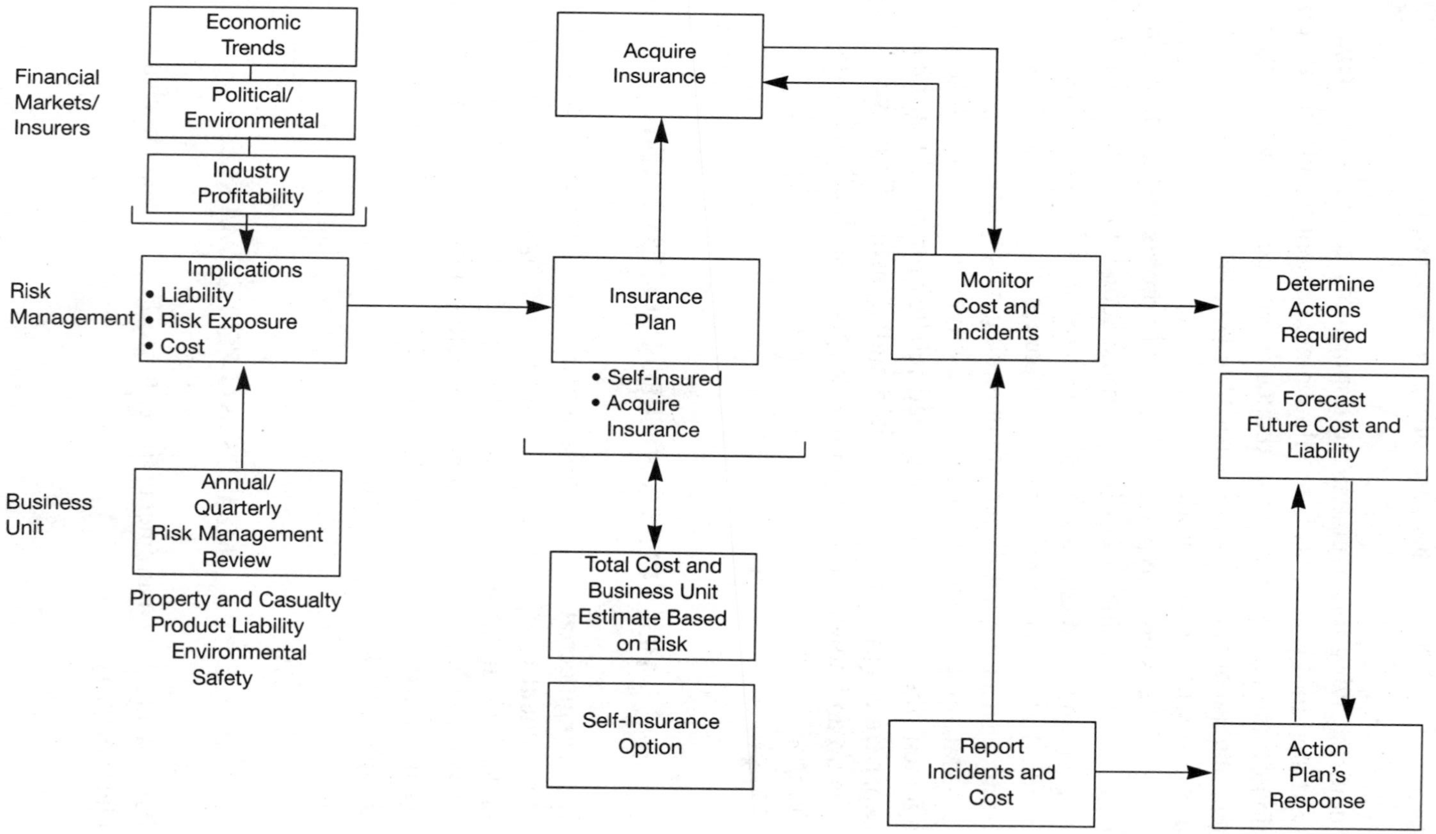

**Exhibit 19-2   Performance Measures:
Risk Management**

Cost Drivers
Number of claims
Legal complexity of claim

Productivity Measures
Number of claims
Average dollar value of claims
Highest dollar value of claims/shareholder equity
Number of insurance carriers
Number of insurance policies

Measures/Quality
Cycle time for settlements
Cycle time for cost recovery
Risk management planning and long-term forecasting
Cycle time for policy acquisition
Total dollar value of claims/ shareholder equity
Historical dollar amount of losses/year (covered by insurance)
Dollar amount of claims processed
Assignment of insurance cost based on business unit risk
Business units
The amount of self-insurance

(a)   COST DRIVERS

The majority of cost drivers are triggered by external events. This explains the strong efforts by corporations to push Congress for regulatory and legal reform. Key cost drivers include:

- New litigation
- New government regulations
- Legal rulings or major settlements
- Product defects
- Environmental or workplace hazards

(b) PRODUCTIVITY MEASURES

Claim volume is the best indicator of risk management productivity. Proactive efforts to manage risk can best be measured by the results of these efforts—the change in the volume and value of claims. The greater the claim value the greater the resource requirement to manage a legitimate claim.

(c) QUALITY MEASURES

Planning and operating and business accountability are essential to managing a world-class risk management process. Measurements that are indicators of a quality process include:

- The level of risk to shareholder equity
- Assigning the cost of managing risk to the units based on risk profile
- Relative operating management accountability for risk

19.7 KEY CHALLENGES

The major challenge for risk management is to shift accountability for risk management to those who have control over risk. Allocations of insurance cost discourages management diligence over managing risk. Lack of diligence can lead to the big surprises, where the liability exposure could put a company out of business.

The more management is given a sense of control over the cost of risk, the more attention will be paid to proactive management of risk.

As has been seen throughout this section, the success of treasury management is dependent on the overall competence and capabilities of finance and general management. It was discussed earlier how treasury processes can contribute to the better management of the business, but treasury is still dependent on the rest of the finance organization to make it a reality.

Treasury has historically been frustrated by the lack of discipline over financial plans and forecast. This has led treasury to discount financial and business information provided by the controller's organization and to prepare its own forecast and analysis for managing cash, working capital, and capital structure.

One of the major themes throughout this book has been the need to empower management and hold it accountable for delivering results. This must also be a major theme for treasury in conducting its business. Treasury is in the financial services business and must come to treat the organizations they support as customers that must be charged for the services provided. All of the responsibilities in the treasury organization could be outsourced to financial institutions. In fact, in most small companies there is no formal treasury function.

In larger companies the financial institutions are aggressively marketing cash management and financial risk management services and products. Investment bankers can take full responsibility for helping the chief financial officer evaluate capital structure and financing strategies, including working capital requirements. Consulting firms specializing in financial risk and insurance can provide financial management with all the services required to replace treasury's responsibility.

On the other hand, this book has discussed how a world-class treasury organization can maximize shareholder wealth. This requires a process management approach where treasury activities are seamlessly integrated into the major financial process they support. This also will require that all physical and professional barriers that separate treasury from the rest of finance be eliminated.

Treasury staff must become active and approachable team players who work closely with all members of the financial community. This will assure that the voice of the shareholder is heard and understood by all members of the finance organization. The voice of the shareholder combined with opportunity to leverage finance's efforts to improve financial performance will encourage all members of the finance community to work with treasury.

Finally, the ultimate test of the success of treasury and, in turn, financial management is the increase in shareholders' wealth. Treasury, along with the entire finance organization, must work diligently to instill in the corporation the value of creating shareholder wealth.

Index

Index

Index

Index

Index

Index

Index

Index

Index

Index

Index

Index